D0969196

THE DON'T SWEAT GUIDE
TO TAXES

Other books by the editors of Don't Sweat Press

The Don't Sweat Affirmations
The Don't Sweat Guide for Couples
The Don't Sweat Guide for Graduates
The Don't Sweat Guide for Grandparents
The Don't Sweat Guide for Parents
The Don't Sweat Guide for Moms
The Don't Sweat Guide for Weddings
The Don't Sweat Guide to Golf
The Don't Sweat Stories
The Don't Sweat Guide to Travel
The Don't Sweat Guide to Weight Loss

THE DON'T SWEAT GUIDE
TO TAXES

**Avoiding Stress
over April 15th**

By the Editors of Don't Sweat Press
Foreword by Richard Carlson, Ph.D.

New York

This book is not intended to offer specific legal, tax, accounting, or financial advice. Readers should consult with their tax preparers, as the tax code can change each year.

Hyperion books are available for special promotions and premiums. For details contact Hyperion Special Markets, 77 West 66th Street, 11th floor, New York, New York, 10023, or call 212-456-0100.

ISBN: 0-7868-8812-1

FIRST EDITION

10 9 8 7 6 5 4 3 2 1

Contents

Foreword

For many people, there are few subjects more stressful or intimidating than taxes! Shortly after the first of the year, up until the final day, there is plenty of anxiety, dread, and stress. The word "deadline" takes on a new significance as "tax day" approaches. When you turn on the radio, you hear all sorts of experts giving out tips.

For bookkeepers, accountants, tax attorneys, and CPAs, the days and nights are long. For the rest of us, there is paperwork to find, rules to sift through, and procrastination to avoid! I'm guessing that a vast majority of people are completely honest, yet most people worry about accuracy and audits. There's no denying the fact that taxes are complicated. I've even heard stories about people calling the Internal Revenue Service for advice, and receiving conflicting advice!

Sometimes, when you hear about all the new tax laws from an expert—even when it's good news—it can make you feel even more stressed. After all, now there are even more factors to take into consideration. It seems that what we really need is a way to get it done right—but to somehow be able to take it in stride.

The editors of Don't Sweat Press have put together a very helpful guide to getting through your taxes. Unlike the vast numbers of technical books, however, this one is geared toward your sanity. It offers simple, practical ways to keep your taxes from overwhelming you—or getting you down. It was written to enhance your perspective and to help keep you from worrying or fretting.

Of course, it's not only April 15 and income taxes that concern people, but the ongoing barrage of other taxes, as well. In a way, every "season" is tax season. Unfortunately, if you think about it too much, it can become overwhelming and can begin to dominate your attention. This book addresses that day-to-day sense of being overwhelmed. It offers tips that encourage us to do what's necessary, but at the same time, to keep our bearings. It helps us to keep from exacerbating the problem with needless worry and agitation. The book reminds us that we are always at our best when our perspective is heightened.

There's an old saying, "There are only two certainties in life—death and taxes." This book will help you make peace with one of those "certainties." While we will never see the day when taxes aren't an integral part of life, we may discover a time when it doesn't have to be quite as stressful. This book may be just what you need to point you in that direction. Good luck with your taxes!

Richard Carlson
Benicia, California
March 2002

THE DON'T SWEAT GUIDE
TO TAXES

1.

Smile! It's Tax Time

Say the word "taxes" and you evoke an almost universal response—fear and loathing. We loathe the notion of giving a big chunk of our hard-earned money to the government, and we fear the consequences of improper filing, or of not having enough money to pay our tax bills. This is why the most important thing that you can do when dealing with taxes is to develop the proper attitude. If you can achieve the right mental approach to taxes, the fear and loathing—and the associated stress—will disappear.

The tax bite can be painful, particularly because taxes are omnipresent. We pay them to all levels of government. Any time that you make a purchase, from an expensive home to a bauble at the five-and-dime, you pay sales taxes. Hop on a plane, and you may pay a boarding fee, which is a type of tax. Realize a bequest, and you pay inheritance taxes. Watch cable TV in the comfort of your home, and you most likely pay a franchise fee to your municipality—still another form of tax.

Rather than allow yourself to buckle under the weight of taxes, you may find it uplifting to think about the services and improvements that our taxes underwrite. Just as patriotism is the emotional foundation of our union, taxes provide the financial pillar for our democracy. It's our tax revenue that finances the construction and maintenance of our highways, our schools, our fire and police protection, our armed forces.

Nobody likes paying taxes, but look out your window as you read this. The tree-lined streets free of garbage, the community parks, and the youth programs are what our taxes provide.

There is an old joke about the fellow who tried to pay his taxes with a smile...but they wanted cash! If we remember all of the benefits that our taxes buy, we can afford ourselves the luxury of feeling less stressed come tax time.

2.

Tax Stats

As a nation of taxpayers, we generate some awesome statistics—"stats," as they're known in the sporting world. The Internal Revenue Service (IRS) generates a statistical snapshot of tax-paying America; here are some of the most interesting findings for the year 1998.

In 1998, 88 million filed taxes. As a group, their tax liability totaled $380 billion, or an average tax liability of $4,310.

Small businesses and self-employed persons grew in great number, reaching a tax liability of $790 billion. This works out to an average tax liability of $20,231 per filer.

The numbers seem daunting, yet several stats in the report suggest that the whole tax affair is neither as intimidating nor as time-consuming as many of us fear. Taxpayers whose income came exclusively or primarily through wages and investments had to deal with an average of only 1.1 tax forms. Little paperwork burden to worry about there! In contrast, large and midsized businesses submitted an average of 3.5 forms, the highest for any group. This group, by the way, also had the highest average tax liability—more than $2.2 million.

In the group declaring principally wages and investment income, fifty-nine percent prepared their own returns, a pretty fair indication that many Americans have a firm handle on their filing and tax obligations.

Impressive as the tax collection statistics may be, the most awesome numbers describe taxes that aren't collected. The IRS estimates that in 1998, the gap between taxes owed and taxes paid was $278 billion. Even that's only a best guess, as there is no real way of knowing the size of the "underground economy" in America. Of all the tax stats, that one may be the most meaningful—and scary.

3.

Where the Money Goes

The federal government allocates tax revenue in a variety of ways, but you may be surprised at the top categories for expenditures. According to the Tax Foundation, in fiscal year 2002, Social Security ranked first (twenty-three percent), with healthcare and Medicare (twenty-two percent) in the second spot. National defense is also important, but at sixteen percent, it's only third on the list.

Other categories commanding large shares of federal spending are income security (fourteen percent), net interest (ten percent), education and training (four percent), transportation (three percent) and veterans' benefits and services (three percent). If you don't see your favorite category here, it's probably lumped in with "other" (six percent).

The debate over budget allocations is one of our most important discussions as a society. It should be thorough, and it should include input from a broad variety of sources. If it does, we don't have reason to question the process—even though we might want a bigger piece of the spending pie for our pet projects.

Any society organized around federal principles must base its budget on prioritized needs of the country as a whole and worry less about the geography of spending. Focusing on the small picture of what your tax payments provide is an example of the kind of thinking that most Americans indulge in at tax time. Changing your way of thinking will help relieve the mental burden that you experience at tax time. As you learn not to stress about taxes, you'll begin taking a more global view and asking, "Are our spending priorities right as a country?" That's a big picture to consider.

4.

I Declare—It's the Best Approach

In 2002, alarmed by what it perceived as a growth in understatement of earnings on the federal tax returns of Americans, the IRS implemented a special program of random audits and tax-return checks. This was necessary, the IRS said, because under-reporting of income cost the federal government $278 billion for the 1998 tax year alone. It's no wonder that the government would like to get a handle on under-reporting.

Unwittingly, even those of us who never file "creatively" may be contributing to this "underground economy." Remember that occasion when you hired a worker for some improvements around the house, and he asked to be paid in cash? When you complied, you gave him the opportunity to omit that income from his earnings report; without a check or credit card statement, there was no record of the transaction. Perhaps you've even been on the other end of the equation, accepting cash for services that you provided, then neglecting to report the proceeds as income.

Aside from the dubious legality of these transactions, there are implications of this underground economy. If you're on the paying end of one of these transactions, you hardly can claim it as a tax credit—that would provide some record of the transaction and imperil the beneficiary, who could then be asked to explain why he didn't report the income that you claimed as a credit.

If you're on the receiving end, you'll never know if the customers who paid you in cash reported that payment on their taxes. You'll always be in danger of being requested by the government to explain the discrepancy.

Perhaps more importantly, under-reporting of income, and the subsequent tax gap that results, violate the spirit of our approach to revenue and services. Our tax rates are graduated so that those who can afford to pay more are asked to do so. Widespread under-reporting of income throws that fair-minded system out of balance, placing a disproportionate burden on those who report their income accurately.

If every taxpayer were to declare all income, the system would work so much better. Think of it this way. If that missing $278 billion could be collected, wouldn't some of it find its way into your life through more and improved services in your community?

5.

Let Us Now Quote the Famous

It was Benjamin Franklin who first noted that nothing is certain in life but death and taxes. While that still may rank as the most enduring comment about taxes, many thinkers—both famous and infamous—have put pen to paper over the years to describe their feelings about taxes.

Ronald Reagan once described taxpayers thusly: "A taxpayer is someone who works for the federal government but who doesn't have to take a civil service examination." A government of the people, by the people, and for the people supports this ideal. We are all working members of our nation.

Some of the sharpest observations about taxes have been tinged with cynicism bordering on bitterness. Consider this remark by Plato: "When there is an income tax, the just man will pay more and the unjust less on the same amount of income."

Or this pithy comment by economist Adam Smith: "There is no art which one government sooner learns from another than that of draining money from the pockets of the people."

The entertainer Arthur Godfrey expressed much the same view, but tempered it with gentle humor. "I'm proud to be paying taxes in the United States," Godfrey said. "The only thing is, I could be just as proud for half the money."

Taxes even have worked their way into literature, such as this excerpt from Margaret Mitchell's *Gone With the Wind*: "Death, taxes, and childbirth! There's not any convenient time for any of them."

Here's a lament that may be the most frightening of all: "The hardest thing in the world to understand is income tax." It was uttered by none other than Albert Einstein. If he had trouble grappling with his taxes, it's no wonder that they're so vexing for us.

As for an appropriate modern tax philosophy, how about this from the G.E. Financial Learning Center: "Though we all must pay taxes, there is no patriotic reason to pay any more than your fair share."

That could be a credo for our times: Pay what you must, fully and promptly—it's the only fair way—but take advantage of every opportunity that the law allows.

6.

Your Attitude Can Be the Enemy

Every so often, we read of some outraged taxpayers whose fury takes a bizarrely original turn—they get a couple million pennies and use them to pay their tax bills. Or they write their tax checks on their bed sheets and submit them to perplexed IRS clerks. If you've ever felt moved to perform one of these acts of near-defiance, your attitude is your enemy—and a powerful enemy it can be.

If you view taxes as an injustice being perpetrated upon you, remember their purpose—to underwrite services for the common good of society. Shaping a new, productive tax attitude is an important goal of your tax process. You're the one in charge, not the victim of any conspiracy, and your goal is to fulfill your obligations as a citizen and still come away in the best possible financial shape.

Once you recast your tax attitude, that very attitude will energize you. You'll take on tax-related chores with enthusiasm because you'll know that you can apply your talents to those tasks. You'll be as creative as the penny-packers, but a whole lot more productive.

7.

Factor Taxes into Your Budget

For most of us, budgeting is pure drudgery. Developing a monthly household spending plan appears to be a time-consuming task, and sticking to it seems to be an invitation into a financial straitjacket. As your new attitude about taxes evolves, it may be useful to discard such stereotypical notions about budgeting.

Refocus your thinking about budgets to reflect a more positive outlook. It's true that adherence to your budget may force you to rein in some discretionary spending, but if you're able to do that, you'll be making progress toward your most important goals. Your aspirations may be to own your own home, save money for your children's education, and take a dream vacation. Budgeting will help you save money for those goals. If you don't save money through budgeting, how else will you, realistically, ever finance your dreams?

Budgeting has never been easier. Many budget templates are available in books and online. You'll find fill-in-the-blanks budget formats and sample budgets emphasizing different priorities for different ages and lifestyles. If you assemble your household bills, you can fill in a template with an evening's work and have a budget format that will serve you well forever.

Whether you adapt your budget from an existing source or create your own format, remember that taxes should be a line item in your spending plan. Last year's taxes are a good starting point from which to estimate this year's taxes. Factor in the whole tax load—federal, state, and local obligations—and build in any modifications related to changes in your income.

To budget for taxes most effectively, you'll need to know the applicable rates of the various taxing bodies. You can either pull this information from last year's returns, or speak to your local government tax office and the local branch of the IRS.

When you factor taxes into your budget, you'll get an immediate feel for what this year's obligation will be—and how much you may need to save to make your tax payment. Budgeting for taxes will smooth out the road ahead and get you closer to your overall life goals.

8.

Saving Now Will Help Later

If you factor taxes into your budget, and you modify that budget as your projected earnings and expenses increase or decrease, you'll have a fairly accurate idea of what your total tax bill will be. You're ready to build on that knowledge and develop a plan for acquiring the funds that you'll need to meet your obligation.

Some tax professionals calculate that about forty percent of your gross income will go to taxes. That figure comes from adding federal, state, and local taxes, but it shouldn't be viewed as exact. Many factors, such as the size of your withholding, the value of deductions that you take, and the tax rates in your state and community, can affect your ultimate tax obligation. It's not uncommon for those who itemize deductions and expenses to see that figure shrink to thirty percent, twenty percent, or even less.

Be that as it may, let's use forty percent of your gross income as the working model for your annual tax obligation. If your employer is withholding, say, twenty-eight percent of your income, it's reasonable to expect that you'll come up short if you rely on withholding alone to get the job done. And if you have income from other sources that isn't subject to withholding—interest income, for example—your shortfall will grow.

If you don't adequately plan for this shortfall, you may need to hunt for cash when it's time to write that tax check. The beginning of spring usually signals the cash-for-taxes scramble that we always see at about that time. Even if you make it, you may be forced to borrow money or prematurely liquidate some of your assets to do so. Neither of these is a happy event.

A better idea is to begin saving for taxes now. If you've included taxes in your budget, look at the line item for your projected taxes for the year. Subtract any taxes paid through withholding. The difference is the amount that you must raise to avoid scrambling. If you divide the amount by twelve, you'll know what you must save each month to meet your goal.

The monthly amount that you must set aside can be much less intimidating than the entire sum that you will owe at year's end. Organizing your savings needs into manageable chunks makes the goal realistic and achievable. You'll enjoy the pleasures that spring will bring, rather than dreading the change of season once again.

9.

Don't Let Taxes Spoil Your Dreams

There is a danger of focusing so much of our energy on taxes that we fail to take advantage of financial opportunities that come our way. As we build expertise and gain confidence in our financial know-how, taxes can play a disproportionate role in our thinking and even cloud our judgment.

Do what's right for you—professionally and personally—with taxes being secondary in your assessment of financial opportunities. If your decisions make you more successful, they'll generate enough income so that taxes will become a secondary concern.

This is not to say that tax considerations can't play a role in your professional deliberations. They can and should. Imagine for a moment that you're the CEO of a large company contemplating relocation. A number of states have submitted handsome proposals to lure you; it's your job now to evaluate them.

What kinds of factors will you look at? The tax rates and any proposed tax abatements, to be sure. But you'll have plenty of other factors to weigh, such as the suitability of the sites for your operations, the state of existing infrastructure and costs to improve it, the proximity of transportation, the availability of a ready workforce, and many others. Tax issues play a role, but they're part of a much more complex decision-making process.

Apply that same thinking to your personal situation. What are your grandest dreams? These dreams may seem unrealistic to you now. It's the nature of dreams to be unrealistic—and it's the nature of humans to pursue them and achieve them nonetheless.

Don't let taxes spoil your dreams. Keep dreaming big, and keep achieving big.

10.

Understanding Tax Tradeoffs

Most major decisions in our lives involve tradeoffs. We find terrific jobs, but they involve lengthy commutes marked by lousy roads and heavy traffic. We locate our dream homes, but they're on private roads that aren't maintained by municipal government. We find cars that make us feel like kings of the road, but they're relentless gas guzzlers. And so we're forced to make choices, getting what we want at the price of things that we don't want.

Your tax situation is no different. You'll find tradeoffs just about every step of the way. For example, you may find the ideal community for you and your family, only to discover that the local tax rates are substantially higher than in communities that you find less desirable. When pondering location decisions, it's not uncommon for large employers to shop for states that offer the most attractive corporate tax packages and rates. As individuals, we're confronted by that same type of location tradeoffs.

Other common financial tradeoffs include falling in love with a house that has an assessed value so high that you'll pay a significant premium in taxes if you choose to buy that residence. Or raising funds to finance a vacation by selling off an asset—generating a tax bill on the gains.

In such tradeoff situations, what is really at stake are your goals. What do you value the most, and what are you willing to trade off to achieve those goals? In the case of that new home, is residential perfection so important to you that you're willing to trade off some of your financial security to get it? Or is accumulating money so vital to you now that you'll accept residing in a less agreeable home, if only temporarily?

Tradeoff decisions are unavoidable—they're much worse if we don't realize the implications of our choices—and there are no right or wrong answers. What's important is to understand and prioritize your goals. It's those goals that should drive your decisions and resulting tax implications, not the reverse.

11.

You're a Trendsetter!

Whatever else they may do, taxes provide documentation of our earnings and expenses. If you want to know if a particular year was good to you, and your memory has blended many years into one, just fish out your federal income tax return for that year. You'll have a comprehensive record of what you made and what you spent—that should sharpen your memory.

This assumes, of course, that you're preserving copies of all of your filings—something you ought to be doing in any case against the possibility of an audit. But previous years' returns provide a much stronger benefit than that. If you review the last five years' returns, for example, you'll get a look at your own personal trends.

You may not think of yourself as having trends in the personal and professional aspects of your life. Most of the time, we're too close to our own decisions and actions to see the patterns that we create. But just as we have tendencies and predilections in our personalities, we have trends in our finances.

Spread out those returns and you'll see, for example, your earnings performance over the past five years. Have your earnings gone up or down? Can you identify the reasons for any trend, and can you implement whatever changes it would take to turn the curve upward?

See if you can spot trends in your expenses, as well. This is easier to do if you're itemizing your deductions. If you observe increases or decreases in your spending, have they been commensurate with changes in your income? If not, can you make the adjustment?

How about your charitable contributions? The gross amount may have changed from year to year, but has the percentage of your income that you're donating to charity remained roughly constant? You even can compare the percentage of your income that's been paid in taxes. If the percentage has increased, you can resolve to be more thorough in your tax planning.

Whether you know it or not, you're a trendsetter. Your tax returns will help you identify your life trends; a wonderful if unintended benefit of our tax system.

12.

The Lottery: Uncle Sam Wins

When you play the lottery, it would be wise to remember that Uncle Sam is your silent partner. No, he didn't pitch in the ten dollars when you collected from everyone in your lottery group, and you don't recall faxing him your numbers. But he's your partner just the same, waiting to collect his share of any winnings.

If the lottery winnings of you or your group exceed five thousand dollars, the state—it doesn't matter which state—is required to withhold a portion for federal taxes. In 2002, the withholding rate was twenty-seven percent, down from twenty-eight percent several years before. For this reason, it's important for you to keep accurate records of who's participating in your group, and to ensure that each group member receives the appropriate share. If you claim the winnings as your own, even if your intention is to distribute shares to all of your partners, you could face the entire tax burden alone.

Remember also that while money is withheld for federal taxes, the same isn't true for state and local taxes. For those taxing bodies, your winnings are viewed as ordinary income and subject to standard tax rates. So it's a good idea to set aside a portion of your winnings to satisfy the state and local tax hit.

Other gambling income is treated similarly. If you win more than five thousand dollars on a two-dollar bet at the racetrack, for example, that same twenty-seven percent will be withheld. An added wrinkle occurs if you win between six hundred and five thousand dollars on a two-dollar bet. The track won't withhold any money, but it is required to notify the IRS. As with lottery winnings, there's no withholding for state and local taxes.

It's wise to be aware of these tax consequences, but none of it should diminish your joy of a big day at the track or a lottery score. If you hit, feel free to whoop, hug, and holler. You've already paid the biggest part of your taxes for this bill.

13.

The States of Taxes

We focus most of our attention on federal income tax. That makes sense, since it's the biggest bite for most of us. In their way, however, state and local levies can be even more interesting and complex. The range of taxes and their rates is almost limitless, making comparisons a risky proposition at best.

Most states impose graduated tax rates on income, but the number of brackets varies considerably. Hawaii, for example, offers nine tax rates, with the top rate kicking in at $40,000 in income. Pennsylvania imposes a flat tax rate of 2.8 percent for all income levels. States such as Colorado, Indiana, and Illinois also maintain a single rate, but it's based on a flat percentage of federal taxable income. These rates range from 3 percent to 4.63 percent. Still a number of other states—Alaska, Florida, Nevada, South Dakota, Texas, Washington, and Wyoming—impose no state income tax.

Differences in tax structures and rates don't begin to describe the colorful panorama of state taxes exclusive of other levies such as sales taxes! Some states, such as New Hampshire and Tennessee, apply their income tax only to interest and dividend income. Others, including Arkansas and California, have assessed their top marginal tax rates to match the rate of inflation. Idaho assesses each filer ten dollars for its permanent building tax fund.

Ohio offers one of the most unusual income tax provisions of all. Whenever the Buckeye State ends its fiscal year with a significant surplus, the excess is refunded to taxpayers through temporary reductions in income tax rates. You can check out state tax rates at the web site of the Tax Foundation, www.taxfoundation.org.

Taxes at the municipal level defy easy summation. Here, you find real estate taxes that may be levied by your county, municipality, school district, or any combination thereof. Occupation taxes—for the right to work in that municipality—are common. Home sales may generate transfer taxes. The range of taxes applied to businesses at the state and local levels may be even wider.

The most important point to be made here is that the total tax package for any community is likely to include many components. If you intend to base your location decision on taxes, you'll need to consider the complete tax package of all of your candidate communities. Pick the community that offers you the most advantages, such as superior schools, proximity to your job, and access to affordable public transportation. Compared to those major amenities, taxes are minor considerations.

14.

Out-of-State Taxes

Imagine that you have a job that takes you from state to state, working in each place temporarily and then moving on. At the end of a long fiscal year, you sit down with your accountant, who reminds you that you're now liable for income taxes in each of the states in which you worked. You may have tax obligations in several of the cities in which you worked, as well.

One of the ramifications of our great mobility as a society is that taxing bodies want to catch up with us for any and all money that we earn in their jurisdictions. The drive for state and local taxation of nonresident earnings has been fueled in recent years by the soaring salaries of professional athletes. In response, local taxing authorities have joined their state brethren in imposing taxes on nonresident workers to claim what they regard as their fair share of athletes' bounty. Since taxes must be applied uniformly, all nonresident workers are liable.

If you earn money in another state, you may be subject to a

variety of state and local taxes. If you're hired to work at the Kentucky Derby, for example, you're now subject to the Louisville/Jefferson County Annual Business Net Profit Occupation License Fee. It may be an obscure tax, but it's now your tax.

Athletes and performing artists feel the sting of nonresident taxes most severely; they're peripatetic by job description. Most of us don't face this challenge to the same degree, and there is some relief. Many states have adopted reciprocal exemptions with neighboring states to ease the burden on residents on all sides of the shared borders. Pennsylvania, for example, has such an agreement with Indiana, Maryland, New Jersey, Ohio, Virginia and West Virginia— even though some of its partners aren't contiguous to Pennsylvania.

If you work frequently in several or more tax jurisdictions, you might want to keep a diary of where you are each day of the year. With that as your base, you and your accountant can determine what percentage of your income was earned in each jurisdiction, as well as the corresponding taxes.

Don't let this challenge stifle your wanderlust. If you have the chance for professional travel, go for it. You don't want to lose that opportunity for what amounts to a bookkeeping exercise, albeit an important one.

15.

When Higher Taxes Are Good News

At tax time, it helps to remember that if your tax obligation has increased from the previous year, it's usually because you're enjoying more income. That's a situation to which most of us aspire. Higher taxes are a price that we pay for greater success, but tax worries never should diminish our enjoyment of our success—or our personal and professional ambition.

We see a similar duality in other tax-related areas, such as the assessment of our homes for tax purposes. Of course it's no fun if your assessment increases and you're stuck with higher property taxes. Yet the revised assessment also means that the value of your home has appreciated, and that you'll realize a greater profit if you decide to sell. It also means that you have more borrowing power—through a line of equity credit, for example—because of your home's enhanced value. The advantages may well outweigh the extra taxes that you'll now be paying.

Higher taxes can be a good thing when they imply growing income for you and your family. You wouldn't want the reverse situation, where declining income brings you a smaller tax bill. That wouldn't be much of a victory.

About the only time that higher taxes are bad news is if you don't increase your tax savings to underwrite your new obligations. When your income rises, make this routine adjustment and all of the news will continue to be good.

16.

Set Aside Time for Your Preparations

One of the reasons that we find taxes so stressful is that we often don't factor tax preparation into our busy schedules. We know that we have to do it, we say that we're going to do it, we assure our spouses that we'll get to it soon. Then "soon" somehow never materializes, and we find ourselves staring down the barrel of the April 15 deadline.

A much less stressful approach is to develop a schedule for the different phases of tax preparation. On a legal pad, jot down the various tasks associated with completing your returns. You should have bullet points for consulting with your team of tax experts, gathering all of the documentation that you need (which should be readily accessible in your files), calculating the preliminary figures, meeting with your tax preparer, and finally, completing and submitting your return packages, including signed returns and checks.

If you spread these tasks over the ten weeks from January 1 to March 15, you'll have ample time to complete each of them and still leave yourself a comfortable cushion of one month before the ultimate deadline. When you view tax preparation as a ten-week process, you'll find that you have plenty of time to accomplish your tasks without a high level of anxiety. Even if you allow a generous amount of time for your tasks—say, four weeks to gather documents and two weeks to solicit input from your tax team—you can meet the deadline with no sweat. If you build plenty of time into your schedule, you'll avoid most of the anguish, as well.

You must be firm in one area. If you establish a specific time as your available window for document gathering, stick to your plan. Once you start pushing it back a day here and a week there, you're on the slippery slope of procrastination, and you may not regain your momentum.

17.

Take a Forward Look

In the corporate world, large companies may spend two or three months developing their budgets for the next year. The draft typically goes through multiple changes—and multiple levels of approval—before it's finalized and ready for implementation. Even then, the budget remains a working document.

Periodically during the year, companies take what they call a "forward look," comparing their revenues and expenses to date to the totals that they've projected and budgeted for the entire year. If they notice any significant negative variances, they may take immediate corrective action—a company-wide austerity plan, for example, or an advertising campaign to boost revenues.

You can successfully adapt the "forward look" concept to your tax-planning process. At the end of each quarter, specify a convenient date, and review your revenue and expenses for the previous three months. Are they in line with what you've projected, or are there variances? Two key measures to look for: Have you earned more than you projected you would, which would tend to increase your tax obligation for that year? And have you accrued enough money to cover your projected tax obligation?

When you take your forward looks, you may be pleasantly surprised to find that all is going as you projected, and that you won't experience a cash shortfall when your tax bills are due. But if your forward look reveals a problem, you'll be able to implement timely changes.

For example, if your income has been unexpectedly high—perhaps you received a bonus that isn't fully covered by the amount withheld for taxes—you can begin putting a little something extra away each month to account for the unexpected increase in your tax obligation. Or you can make up the shortfall on the spending end, forgoing certain discretionary expenses, and thereby increasing the amount that you can save.

Forward looks work in tax planning—and in other areas of goal achievement. Looking forward involves a couple of the basic questions that we want to ask of all our goals: Where are we now? And if we're off track, how do we get back on our path?

18.

Meeting Deadlines,
Preventing Dreadlines

April 15 is the deadline for our income taxes, but that doesn't mean that we're required to file our returns on That Very Day! It's a deadline all right, but there's no reason to turn it into a dreadline. Instead, think of it as a key date in a year-round tax plan.

Look at some of the achievements in your life that involved planning. You've conceived and planned projects for your career. If you're married, you've participated in the planning for a wedding. You were able to plan successfully for these events because you saw them as dynamic processes, rather than as feats to be pulled off in a single day.

Approach your taxes in the same way. Develop a year-round tax plan. The first phase will be preserving and filing all income statements and any expenditures that could be related to taxes. These will be especially important if you itemize your deductions, or if you're self-employed and taking deductions for business expenses. Save records for any home improvement costs; for your automobile, if you use it for business; for entertainment, if the entertainment is for professional purposes; and for your cell phone, if you use it for business reasons. All of these expenses can be deductible in certain cases.

Filing your tax documents is also a very important aspect of record-keeping. Use a fireproof file cabinet for the job. If you have many tax records, you may want to use multiple files. For example, you may want to have one file for "home improvements," perhaps another for "charitable contributions," and so on.

The next phase is accruing funds for any tax bill. You may not know exactly what your final tax bill will be, but your experience from previous years will give you a rough idea. If you set aside money according to a schedule, the bite won't be as sharp later on.

By January 31 of any given year, you should have all of your documents in order and in hand. Any employer or client who owes you an income statement will have delivered it by then. Now, you're set to use the month of February and the first part of March to develop your preliminary tax returns, working with your tax preparer, if you engage one.

By March 15, you'll have your preliminary returns in hand. You'll have a full month to finalize them and identify ways of financing any obligation. Essentially, you're done. Thanks to your conscientiousness, you're a full month ahead of the deadline, and you've avoided the stress that most people associate with taxes—all because you've planned for it.

19.

Taxes Mean Trust

If you file taxes jointly with your spouse, one of the most significant implications of your filing is trust. When you and your spouse sign your joint returns each year, your signature says that you trust your spouse. You trust the information that your spouse has provided. You trust that the information is complete. You trust that it's accurate. That's why you're willing to sign it. The trust factor in a joint tax filing is as vital as it is unrecognized.

Of course, not all couples file joint returns. The "Married Filing Separately" alternative works for some couples who've kept the bulk of their assets separately titled and might benefit if they file separately. This is an option frequently selected by couples who have specified their individual assets in prenuptial agreements. For other couples, filing a joint return will kick them into a higher bracket. If filing separately will save you money, do it. It does not imply that your relationship is without trust. But if you file jointly, remember that trust is paramount to the proceeding.

20.

Find a Preparer That You Trust

We've seen how taxes rely on the trusting relationship that you have with your spouse. Trust comes into play in another twosome, as well—your relationship with your tax preparer.

Tax calculations are so uncomplicated for some people that they're quite capable of handling the chore themselves. Others with straightforward returns hire one of the national commercial tax-preparation houses for the job. These returns are mostly formulaic; preparation may not require a close, trusting relationship with the person who crunches those numbers.

But if you (and your spouse) have income from multiple sources, or you itemize deductions or have other complicating factors, you want a tax preparer that you can trust. It goes without saying that your tax preparer should have impeccable credentials and solid experience. This is true whether or not your preparer is a certified public accountant (CPA). Anyone, with or without professional training, can prepare and submit a tax return, but CPAs can represent taxpayers before the IRS.

Select a preparer who is familiar with your situation, your goals, your needs, and your finances. In tax-return preparation, chemistry is important. Often, there will be options from which you may choose. For example, should you take a capital gain now or defer it until next year? All of the options will be perfectly legal, yet some will be more beneficial than others. When your preparer recommends courses of action, you want to be comfortable that the suggestions are in your best interests.

Interview several candidates for the job, and ask a series of key questions. What is the fee? If it's an hourly fee, how many hours will the job take? Will your candidate appear with you if you're called in for an audit? Will the candidate handle your account personally, or will it be delegated to someone else in the office? If your account will be delegated, can you interview the person who will handle your return? Is your candidate available for tax advice throughout the year, and if so, what are the charges for those consultations? Will the candidate supply references whom you may contact? If you ask these questions of each candidate, you'll have plenty of information—and a good basis for comparison.

Fair is fair—your preparer has the right to feel comfortable with you, as well. The best situation is when you interview your prospective preparer and your preparer asks questions of you. The give-and-take will be productive. You'll get to know each other. You'll establish that mutual comfort zone that will lead to tax submissions that help you achieve your most cherished financial goals.

21.

When to Take Advice,
When to Reject It

Because taxes are such a universal experience, almost everyone has been through the drill and formed some definite opinions on the best way to go about things. As a result, whether you solicit it or not, you're likely to receive a lot of advice about your taxes.

Some advice will come from professionals—for example, from the accountant who's leading you through the process. You'll always want to consider counsel from experienced professionals. But you'll also get many tips from family and friends. While this coaching may be well-intentioned, it's wise to approach unsolicited advice with a degree of caution.

Of course, your friends have acquired tax experience in some of the same ways that you have, so their advice may make sense for people who share their circumstances. That's just the point. Your circumstances are unique. No matter how similar your situation seems to those of friendly advisors, there are key differences. Few people know exactly what you make, exactly what you spend, whether you itemize expenses, how much is withheld from your pay, or how many deductions you claim. If they're not familiar with these key aspects of your finances, how can they know what tax-planning strategies will work for you?

In addition, they would be even less familiar with your long-term professional and personal goals. Their personal game plan may involve maximizing revenue now to finance immediate objectives. But if you adopt a similar approach, it could lead to tax-planning strategies that lead you astray. If you take advice from these folks, you may well impair your chances of achieving your goals.

Think of unsolicited tax advice in the same way you regard advice in other areas of your life. You never want to ignore advice completely; that would tend to insulate you from the benefits of learning something new. On the other hand, you don't want to accept it uncritically because no one knows better than you what's best for you.

Strike a balance. Review advice carefully, accept what seems to work for you, and reject the rest. Be as diplomatic as you can when you deflect tips from family and friends, but be firm in your resolve.

22.

Build Your Own Team of Experts

The Internal Revenue Code, a.k.a. the Tax Code, can be a daunting document. You can't be expected to know it chapter and verse, and even the most experienced CPAs must study thick bulletins to keep up with annual changes to the code. So how can you be sure that you're complying with the code—to say nothing of the maze of state and local regulations—and taking advantage of all of the tax-saving provisions that may apply to you?

One way is to build a team of experts for your taxes. Your accountant or other tax preparer can be the key player on the team, but remember—accountants may have gaps in their expertise. Your other team members can fill in those gaps.

For example, tax preparers don't deal with insurance policies and issues on a daily basis; they may not know the full range of tax implications associated with certain insurance policies, and they may not be able to recommend concepts that will provide the biggest tax advantages for you. Thus, your team could include an insurance expert.

Experts in investments and estate planning also should be on your team. If you've engaged professionals to help you manage your investment portfolio and craft an estate plan, it's up to you to bring them aboard your tax team.

Think of the power that you can assemble. You could have as many as four or five top professionals collaborating to provide you with the first-rate tax planning that you and your tax preparer might never achieve on your own. You'll find that most professionals will be happy to assist you in this manner—and they may not even charge you extra for the additional advice that you're seeking. They realize that if they satisfy you as a client, they're more likely to retain you as a client.

Regard tax preparation and planning as a team sport. Then it will be a game that you're more likely to win.

23.

You Be the Coach

Many people believe that where taxes are concerned, they are victims, held hostage by an inevitable process that allows them no input, no control. This passive approach becomes something of a self-fulfilling prophecy; where people believe that they lack control, they seldom try to assert control.

If you have the right attitude, taxes won't be something that just happens to you. Taxes are a process, and you're in charge of the process. In sports terms, think of yourself as the coach of the Tax Team. If you prefer a business analogy, you're the leader of an important task force.

What does the coach or leader do? First, you select the most productive members to round out your team. These are the specialists, the contributors who can provide the specific expertise that your team needs. The one prerequisite: All of them must be team players with the best interests of the team at heart.

Next, the team leader solicits input from all teammates.

Everyone will have ideas. Your job as leader is to ensure that all parties have a chance to express their opinions and that the ensuing dialogue is a productive one.

Finally, the team leader assembles the options, selects those that appear to be the best, and begins to implement the game plan. If you've carefully cultivated input from all of your team members, they'll "buy in" to your plan and help you with smooth and timely implementation.

You may be called on for other duties as the leader of your own tax team. You may, for example, have to replace members who no longer can participate, for whatever reason. Or you may want to impose personnel changes because the chemistry on your team just isn't right. Even the best game plans must be modified from time to time in light of changing circumstances; spearheading these modifications will be your job, as well.

If you've regarded yourself as a passive participant in taxes, this leadership role can be invigorating for you—there are other benefits, too. Once you've demonstrated to yourself that you can effectively take charge of taxes, other challenges that may have appeared daunting might become more manageable.

24.

The Value of Communication

Your tax team is like a football squad, where talented specialists put their skills together to form a powerful unit. The comparison to football, or any other team sport, is appropriate in another way. In both cases, regular and clear communication is essential.

Any football fan is familiar with the complex system of communications between coaches and players happening every thirty to forty-five seconds throughout the game. Without tight coordination, the game could not go on—at least in any form that would be recognizable or enjoyable to us.

Your tax planning and preparations require communication that is similarly effective; fortunately, you don't need it twice a minute. But as your team's coach, it's up to you to call the plays and keep the information flowing.

What should your communication efforts include? First, make sure that all of your team members know each other—and that they're all working toward the common goal of the best tax plan for you. Distribute phone and fax numbers, as well as e-mail addresses, of each participant to all team members. An inexpensive kickoff lunch might be a pleasant way to handle the introductions.

Next, make sure that you're in regular touch with your team. Phone and e-mail them. If you encounter newspaper or magazine articles that seem relevant to your situation, clip and copy them and distribute them to your team members. If you have an investment question that would relate to your insurance expert and your accountant, don't hesitate to organize a conference call that brings them both together with you.

Coordinating communications is one of your most important tasks as team leader. If you do it well, your team will develop the habit of communicating effectively and thoroughly.

25.

Seize the Day

You've taken many steps to ensure that you honor all of your tax obligations while providing the most advantageous returns for yourself. You've recruited and assembled a tax team, your own personal elite unit that will fortify you with expert advice on all facets of taxes. You've assigned yourself the role of team coach, keeping all team members active and happy. You've developed the right attitude about advice, listening carefully to all suggestions but accepting only those that make sense for you.

This is all good stuff—congratulations for setting up a great tax apparatus. But your work isn't done. As the team coach, you must be prepared to seize the day to make sure your mechanism functions smoothly and continuously.

Don't await developments—get out ahead of them. Send your team members media dispatches and ask for their feedback. When deadlines are approaching, energize your tax team to make sure that those deadlines are met. Inevitably, the professionals who are helping you are helping others, as well. They may also have their own tax, personal, and professional matters competing for their time. You can keep your issues on the front burner by staying in regular touch with your team.

Some might call this the "squeaky wheel gets the grease" theory of taxes, and there may be some truth to this. But calling attention to your concerns is fair, and you can continue to be nice while you're being persistent.

When we deal with experienced, highly regarded professionals, we're often reluctant to probe, to serve as devil's advocate, or to seek additional opinions. This may be because of the respect that we have for the professionals—and because we recognize that our own expertise in these complex fields may be limited. But your knowledge base has grown considerably; there's no longer any reason to be shy or feel intimidated. When it comes to your own taxes, you're in charge—courteously, of course, but always in charge.

26.

Small Things Count

No matter how complex your particular tax preparations, the process is really a series of small steps. For example, you're on a business trip and the cab driver doesn't have an official receipt form. You can come up with a homemade receipt that the driver can initial or sign. That receipt may be worth only a small amount in your total tax calculations, but if you take fifteen dollars here and twenty dollars there, pretty soon, you're talking real money. Everything counts.

You can use the same thinking with your charitable contributions, provided that you itemize them. Sure, that ten dollars you give to the Daffodil Fund at the office won't get you very far, but if you save all such receipts, it will mean money in your pocket later on.

What you're really doing when you save receipts for even the minutest expenditures is developing an accountant's mindset. If you do it each and every time, it will become a habit that will require little thought. When you file your return, you'll be confident that you're enjoying every advantage to which you're entitled, because you remembered that the small things count.

27.

If You Slip Up, Find a Pickup

When it comes to self-improvement, we tend to be purists. Do these scenarios sound familiar? You miss a day's workout at the gym, so you regard your exercise regimen as hopelessly ruined and revert to your couch-potato ways. After fighting the temptation for months, you give in and devour a slice of that chocolate fudge cake that's been calling your name; your diet, you're convinced, now is wrecked beyond salvation, so you ignore the good nutritional habits that you've worked so hard to develop. Or how about this one: You backslide and enjoy that fateful cigarette. Later, awash in guilt, you determine that your kick-the-habit campaign is a failure, and you become a pack-a-day junkie once more.

While there is something quite admirable in holding ourselves to the highest standards, this approach can be self-defeating. Who can measure up? These are demanding tasks that we've assigned ourselves; small, infrequent mistakes aren't a signal that it's time to abandon the whole project.

The same can be said of saving and preserving tax-related documents on a year-round basis. This is hard work—building and internalizing a new habit—so occasional slipups are inevitable. For example, you make a contribution at your office to the local fund for cancer research but forget to request a receipt, or you get a receipt but toss it away when you empty your pockets or purse.

This should not mark the end of your document-saving effort. Perhaps it's too late to rescue that ten-dollar tax-deductible contribution, but perhaps it isn't. First, you can call the charitable organization and see if they'll provide you with another receipt. Perhaps more importantly, you can use your omission as a reminder to redouble your efforts to collect and save documents.

If you fall into this trap, do something to reinforce your determination and confidence, to regain the proper frame of mind. Take out last year's tax returns and compare your year-to-date earnings with last year's totals. Go through this year's tax documents and begin a preliminary categorization. Touch base with your accountant. These little pickups will help you overcome your slipup and remind you that the goals that you've established for yourself remain achievable.

28.

Develop a Filing Protocol

If you've done all of the right things in preparing your tax returns and you're ready to file, you still have some chores ahead before you're wrapped up for the year. Relax. These are small things compared to what you've achieved so far. But you should develop a filing protocol to make sure that returns arrive at their destinations and are properly credited to your account.

Here's a good drill to follow. First, make sure that you, your spouse, and your tax preparer have signed and dated all applicable returns, and that any checks that you're remitting are legibly written for the proper amounts. Write your Social Security number on each check. Some tax preparers also recommend that you write the relevant tax form number on each check, such as 1040-US for your federal return. These steps may seem tedious and unnecessary, but if your tax payments aren't properly credited to you, you may get a notice from the government asking why you haven't paid. At the very least, use your Social Security number on all checks.

You've taken care of the contents. Now, you're ready for the envelopes. Match your returns with the proper envelopes, and double check the addresses on the envelopes. Add your return address, as well. If you're a veteran tax filer, you know the Murphy's Law corollary that applies to tax returns: The envelopes provided by any government agency are never large enough to contain the forms. You can try to wrestle them into the government-provided envelopes if you like, but you may be better off addressing and using your own envelopes. That way, you'll be pretty sure that no pages will be detached or mutilated in the Herculean stuffing process.

The last part of your protocol will be affixing adequate postage to each envelope before mailing. If it's a thick package, don't guess at the postage. Instead, have it weighed at the post office.

The whole postage business seems like adding insult to injury, doesn't it? Here you are, submitting thousands of dollars to help run our government without so much as a peep of protest, and they're nicking you for postage, too. This type of thinking is a vestige of your old tax attitude. Think of this as your final step in licking the tax challenge. The few pennies that you're spending are a small enough price to pay for successfully meeting the challenge.

29.

Filing in the E-Age

Practically every aspect of American commerce is hip-deep in the e-Age, so it's no wonder that tax filing has gone electronic. The IRS offers an online return submission program known as "e-file" that has considerable appeal for taxpayers who are at ease working with their computers. The e-file option offers a number of advantages. It's touted as a paperless system, meaning that if you file by computer, the IRS will not require some of the usual paperwork backup—including W-2 forms. If your return requires significant paper backup, e-filing probably isn't for you. And if you go this route, don't view it as an excuse for suspending collection, filing, and preservation of tax-related documents. You'll still need those in case of any audit.

If you file your federal taxes electronically, you can simultaneously file your state tax returns in thirty-seven participating states. You'll gain the advantage of a little time, since you can e-file up to the last minute—and without leaving your home. If you have a refund coming, the IRS offers a direct deposit option to e-filers, and it pledges to speed the refund process; you may receive yours in as little as ten days.

You'll need an appropriate software package to file electronically. The IRS doesn't provide that software, but if you visit the IRS web site at www.irs.gov, you'll find a directory of private sector companies that have partnered with the IRS to offer appropriate software packages. Some e-file partners offer their software free of charge, although it is likely that you will get a pitch for consultation and tax-preparation services; with your new attitude about taxes and your expanded information base, you're well positioned to sort out helpful offers from come-ons.

The IRS reports that e-file is both popular and successful—it expected to receive about 45 million online returns in 2002—with an error rate of less than one percent on forms filed electronically. Clearly, e-filing requires a degree of computer sophistication. But if you're up to it, e-filing will help you consolidate your control over your taxes. You'll be in charge of what you file and when you file, and you'll be in direct contact with the IRS. It's yet another way of taking charge of your taxes.

30.

Be Aware of Software

Traditionally, tax preparation has been a manual exercise heavy on paper backup. Perhaps you deployed a calculator to speed the process, but there was little other role for technology. However, now that computers are almost as prevalent as calculators are in the home, online filing has become a viable option for some taxpayers. Now that we're able to file our federal income taxes online, you may want to consider an even broader electronic approach to taxes.

Today, you can acquire a host of commercial software packages for tax preparation; unless your occupation demands customized forms and returns, you probably can find a software package that will help you. Computer-aided preparation can be an asset in several regards.

First, you may be somewhat less likely to make errors when the software is providing the calculations for you. Also, your program can give you a line-by-line listing of the information that you need, reducing the chances that you'll forget any important data. Of course, your tax preparer would probably call any omissions to your attention.

But if you're preparing your taxes online, you can electronically ship your preliminary figures to your tax preparer, obviating the need for face-to-face meetings. If you reduce the amount of "face time" with your preparer, you may enjoy a smaller bill from that professional.

A software package also could enable online filing of your taxes, providing potential time savings and all the advantages of electronic submission. Software packages can help in other ways, as well. You may find a package that combines tax preparation and online banking, for example, bringing you such advantages as round-the-clock access to your bank account information.

If you go the software route, look for packages that are flexible enough to easily accommodate changes in tax rates and laws. When it comes to the Tax Code, change is constant. Software packages must be able to accommodate change or they won't be of continuing use to you.

Not everyone will consider software packages as the tax-preparation mode of choice. But if you're comfortable on the computer and willing to invest in a software package, you'll have yet another weapon in your tax-preparation arsenal.

31.

Extension Prevention

Most of us labor mightily to meet the April 15 deadline for tax-return submission. Nothing is quite so predictable as the hectic scene as T-Day approaches midnight—postal workers on overtime out on the street to collect last-minute returns, good citizens in night clothes waving their returns through open car windows, looking for the first friendly hand, live footage of the chaos on the eleven o'clock news.

And yet, April 15 is not the absolute deadline for federal returns. The IRS does grant extensions for filing the paperwork, although any tax obligation must be paid by April 15. In fact, if you request it, the IRS automatically gives you a four-month extension, no questions asked. You can apply for an additional extension of two months, but the second request is not automatically granted and could be denied.

Certainly, it's easy to envision circumstances when you might need an extension. One can imagine family illnesses that occupy so much of your time that you must suspend your attention to your tax returns. Changes in job, relocations—all can require considerable time and attention on your part, so much so that you might need a filing extension.

Absent these circumstances, however, extensions probably aren't a great idea for you. First, an extension won't provide any grace period on payments—for many the most difficult aspect of the whole process. If you can come up with the cash, the corresponding paperwork should be the easier part of the battle.

Even beyond that, you have a new, can-do attitude about taxes; you'll be ready to submit well before the deadline. Why push it back and rob yourself of the satisfaction that you'll get from on-time completion? Why exchange one deadline for another that may be no more attractive?

Apply for an extension only when family or professional circumstances make it absolutely essential. Otherwise, stay the course!

32.

Taking a Tax Vacation

Inevitably, as you go through the process of consulting with your tax team, preserving all your tax documents, and working through all the levels of tax returns, you'll hit the wall. You'll be fed up with anything related to taxes.

Relax. If you don't let it overwhelm you, the frustration you may be feeling will be temporary. You've undertaken quite a task; it will be many months before the whole scenario plays out. It's natural to feel a little anxiety when you're not yet able to see the benefits of your hard work. Those will come.

When you encounter this frustration, you can try several strategies to get you over the hump. Some folks favor what we might call the "hair of the dog" approach. Frustrated with taxes and knowing they're ready to give up the tax ghost, they dive in even more deeply. They schedule consultations with their tax team and keep all discussions centered on their taxes. They convert informal office meetings to tax harangues. They surf the Internet, looking for tips from the supposed experts.

This total tax immersion may not be for all. For such others, a brief break from all things taxes might be just the tonic. If this sounds like the right approach, get as far away from taxes as you can. Take long walks or engage in more vigorous exercise. Spend time with your kids and spouse. If you espy a tax-related article in the paper, skip it. If a member of your tax team calls, notify your colleague that you're on tax vacation.

Alas, your vacation must be brief—there's still work to be done. But if you're able to take a few days away from all tax discussions and considerations, you should come back fresher—and even more determined to take charge of your taxes.

33.

When You Finish—Celebrate!

As you organize your tax-preparation activities, you'll find that the task falls into natural categories: gathering materials, preliminary calculations, review, final calculations, and submission. It's a great idea to mark the completion of each task group in some way that will have meaning for you.

For some, simply stroking a line through the assignment on a tax to-do list will be reinforcement enough; that simple little stroke for them represents a task completed and well done, even as it provides encouragement to go on to the next job on the list. Others may need a more visible reminder—boldly writing the word "Done!" on a wall calendar, for example—that they've successfully completed the job in the allotted time.

You may prefer something more ceremonial—dinner at a favorite restaurant, perhaps, with a cocktail and a toast to your success. Or you may find that telling others you've completed your task swells your sense of pride.

Do whatever feels right to you, and don't think of your actions as shamelessly self-congratulatory. Recognition of our good work can be nearly as vital as the good work itself. Some type of acknowledgment will reinforce all of the exemplary tax habits that you've developed, and it will inspire you to continue to the next stage of your preparations.

Think of the many types of recognition that have helped you along the way: the report card that showed that you were progressing nicely through your studies; graduation day; outstanding performance reviews at work. All gave you a glow, a sense of pride in your accomplishments—and the determination to extend your record of success.

The difference in tax preparation is that there's no outside agency, no teacher, no boss to confirm how well you've done. The IRS doesn't send congratulatory notes for on-time, accurate submissions.

Rewarding yourself is largely up to you. Do it, and feel good about it. You *need* recognition, whether symbolic or tangible, of your tax accomplishments. The best person to provide that recognition is you.

34.

Taxes: A Brief History

We think of income taxes as an inevitable part of our lives, yet the history of taxes in the United States is evolutionary. In the earliest days of the republic, there was no income tax. For revenue, the federal government relied on a sort of sales tax that was selectively applied to such items as distilled spirits, tobacco and snuff, corporate bonds and—tragically enough—slaves. To help underwrite the costs of the War of 1812, the government imposed sales taxes on a number of additional items—refined sugar, gold, silverware, jewelry, and watches among them. Hard as it may be to believe now, Congress actually repealed all internal taxes in 1817, relying on tariffs on imported goods to pay the freight.

The income tax was implemented in 1861 to help raise revenue for the Civil War, but even this didn't mark its permanent inclusion in the landscape. It was repealed in 1872, revived in 1894, and declared unconstitutional by the U.S. Supreme Court in 1895. It was only in 1913, with the adoption of the Sixteenth Amendment to the Constitution, that the federal income tax was institutionalized.

Inheritance taxes have the same checkered past. They came on the scene relatively late—Congress imposed them in 1916. Now, they're scheduled to be phased out completely by 2010, showing how dramatically a nation may change its tax philosophy.

We can learn several lessons from the evolution of taxes. The first is that the financial needs of war appear to play a major role in the shaping of tax policy. On at least two occasions, war has triggered creation of new taxes. Does it follow that a nation at peace would need fewer taxes, and that tax relief could function as a peace benefit? That's food for thought.

The second conclusion we can draw is that the tax scene will change. It always has changed in the past, and it's likely to change in the future. For us, that means that we need to develop a degree of flexibility in our tax planning and our attitudes about taxes. It's better to understand change and manage it effectively than to be dragged kicking and screaming into a new tax era.

35.

A Tangled Web

As we've seen, taxes in America are a work in progress. Our most widely applied levy, the federal income tax, has been imposed three times and repealed twice, and it's likely that we'll see further evolution. We know that there will be tax-law modifications, because we'll see changes—writ large and small—in the ways that we do business and the ways that we relate to each other. Our tax laws will need to catch up out of necessity.

Consider the area of the Internet. Clearly the framers of tax law couldn't have envisioned the development of cyber-communications, or the role that this new tool would play in commerce. As a result, we've had to revise our tax rules to encompass the New Economy.

Congress took a stab at doing so by imposing a moratorium on taxes for Internet access, a moratorium that was extended by President George W. Bush in 2001. This means that you don't pay taxes on the connectivity that you buy from your Internet service provider—a fair-minded approach, since it helps keep connectivity affordable.

But what about taxes on Internet sales? Given that billions of dollars in goods and services now are purchased online, this is a growing concern. In theory, sales taxes are levied on Internet transactions in the same ways that states impose them on all other sales, be they in stores or through catalogues. In practice, however, there is no law that empowers states to collect taxes from out-of-state e-tailers. When the General Accounting Office took a look at this situation, it projected that by 2003, states could lose $12.5 billion in uncollected taxes on Internet sales.

If you've purchased goods from an out-of-state e-tailer, you've enjoyed an inadvertent benefit; you most likely paid no sales tax on the transactions. Yet with the volume of money at stake, it's hard to imagine that states will tolerate this situation for very much longer.

E-tailers someday may be required to impose and collect sales taxes on all transactions; e-purchasers someday may be required to pay those taxes. That's why a flexible approach to taxes is so important. Tax laws *will* change, and we must be prepared to change with them.

36.

Taxes Around the World

Unless they've lived in several different countries, people tend to think of taxes as a phenomenon exclusive to our nation. Taxes, however, are international, and remain the principal revenue-generating tool for most of the world's countries. A look at taxes around the world provides a glimpse of a colorful and varied landscape—and some method to the madness.

Rates for income taxes vary across a wide range. In Vietnam, for example, the top rate for individual income taxes is sixty percent, while Saudi Arabia imposes a much milder top tax rate of twenty-five percent on individual income. South Africa has installed a maximum tax rate of forty-five percent, while its neighbor, Zambia, maintains thirty percent as the rate for its top bracket.

Perhaps the most interesting aspect of taxes around the world is how national tax codes reflect national priorities. In America, we're accustomed to tax laws that reinforce, among other things, the nurturing of families. Other tax codes have different emphases. In

South Africa, a country of considerable decentralization, local councils are authorized to collect a service tax on business entities within their districts. Greece, which is interested in the economic growth of its small islands, offers tax incentives for hotel and tourism developments on those would-be resort meccas.

Zambia eschews a capital gains tax but does maintain a levy on mineral royalties, reflecting the importance of mining to the Zambian economy. Monaco, a wealthy principality, imposes no individual income tax, but it does collect a gift tax ranging from eight to sixteen percent of declared value. Belarus excuses income taxes on payments received for donations of blood and breast milk.

To a great extent, taxes are nationally and culturally based. In fact, if you want to learn about any country, you can get a good feel for priorities there by reading up on the local tax code.

Tax expertise is also nationally based. Familiarizing yourself with American tax policies won't necessarily help you in other lands. If you're traveling abroad or planning to work temporarily in another country, make sure that you study local tax law—or get some reliable indigenous advice.

37.

Tax Cheats

Everybody will pay taxes, and there will be no exceptions." This quote may sound like a founding father explaining the need for a universal levy, or a senior IRS official introducing a new collection initiative. However, these words were declared by Boris Yeltsin in a 1996 address in which the then-president of Russia announced a crackdown on tax cheats.

What we may conclude from Yeltsin's stern warning is that cheating on taxes is just about as universal as taxes themselves. In Australia, for example, the federal government in 2000 implemented tax policies that it projected would raise seven billion dollars from tax cheats.

In America, the IRS puts the gap between taxes owed and taxes paid at $278 billion for 1998 alone—that's more chasm than gap. It's no wonder that tax authorities have turned to innovative means to narrow the gap.

The state of Illinois, for example, went so far as to publish an online list of state tax scofflaws—a brazen step, considering the risk of litigation that the state was incurring. The 1999 initiative was wildly successful. According to Bankrate.com, public embarrassment induced 903 taxpayers on the list to fork over nearly ten million dollars, while 169 others agreed to installment payment plans worth another nine million dollars.

Our federal government for years has employed a "tip" program that often pays informants for information that leads to successful prosecution of tax cheats. MSN.com indicates that the IRS collects more than $100 million annually as a result of tips, and pays from two million to five million dollars in rewards, although only about eight percent of claims filed since 1960 have resulted in cash awards.

Claiming a reward isn't that easy. You must fill out the appropriate form, and you must identify yourself by name; the IRS pledges not to disclose your identity to "unauthorized persons." Awards can range up to two million dollars but typically are smaller—a percentage of money recovered as a result of your tip.

All of which gives rise to an interesting ethical question: If you're aware of tax cheating, should you report it to the appropriate authorities? You may know how damaging tax cheating is, so you may have strong reasons for blowing the whistle. Yet it's also true that reporting on a suspected tax cheat could lead to an unjustified investigation or prosecution. It's a tough call—one that demands careful deliberation.

What you *can* do about tax cheating is to honor your tax obligations in full. When everyone adopts that approach, we'll no longer have a problem with tax cheating.

38.

Tax Protesters Doth
Protest Too Much

Whether cheerfully or grudgingly, most of us recognize our duty to pay taxes, and most of us fulfill our obligations. The same can't be said of tax protesters, who aren't so much objecting to their specific calculations but are attacking the legal underpinning of the Tax Code.

The attacks come from several directions. Some protesters maintain that the Constitution doesn't specifically authorize the income tax, or that the Constitutional provisions for the income tax never were properly ratified. In this scenario, taxes become an unwarranted and illegal seizure of private property.

Another group attacks from a different flank, going around and around about the legal definitions of such fundamental tax terms as "taxpayer," "person," or "employee." This argument is rooted in semantics and stands little chance of paving the way for any tax changes.

Still other protesters aim their mortars at the definition of "income," suggesting that compensation such as wages and tips don't count as income. Or they claim that only gold or silver currency can be taxed, or that they operate churches and are not subject to taxes. In one of the more creative variations, protesters adjust their income to reflect the declining value of the dollar, wiping out most of their income and taxes.

These challenges don't hold up in court; moreover, should a court find the protest frivolous, it may impose a penalty of up to $25,000. Of course, that fine would be beyond any interest and penalties due if the protester failed to properly file returns and pay taxes.

Most of us never would arrive at such obscure challenges independently, but there are protest groups that recruit members via slick presentations. You may even be asked to pay a fee to join and be given vague promises about a handsome return on investment down the road. If you're asked to join, beware.

Tax protesters doth protest too much. They've been advised time and again that there is no legal basis for their protests. Even beyond that, if they were victorious, what would their spoils be? A nation in turmoil because it lacked the revenue to finance government services? That's hardly a desirable goal.

Tax protesting in our country in the modern era is a tremendous waste of valuable human energy that could be turned to improving public policy on taxes. That's where everyone's involvement would be most helpful.

39.

The Most Famous Tax Protesters

Tax protesters seldom achieve much more than an outrageous bill for unpaid obligations and the threat of some time spent as a guest of the government. On rare occasion, however, tax protesters take a stand that reverberates through the ages.

Such was the case with Lady Godiva. She is, of course, history's most famous nude, whose wild eleventh-century ride has become legend. Less well known about Lady Godiva is that her ride actually was a tax protest.

As the story goes, the good lady was married to the tax collector in the English town of Coventry. When her husband imposed an onerous tax on the town's poorest residents, his wife protested, imploring him time and again to eliminate the levy. Nagged to distraction, the man replied that he would eliminate the tax the day that she rode naked through town.

His challenge may have been more rhetorical excess than an actual proposal, but Lady Godiva treated it as a deal. She made her famous ride, and her husband, good as his word, repealed the tax. In an odd postscript to the story, the old tax collector died soon after the alleged ride, leaving his considerable land holdings to his youngish widow. The lady was transformed from reckless defender of the poor to member of the landed gentry; if she felt bad about taxes on the poor thereafter, there's no record of it.

For all of her presumed selflessness, Lady Godiva may not be history's best-known tax protester. That honor could belong to William Tell, the archer who took bow in hand to shoot an apple from his son's head. Why would he attempt a fool thing like that? It was a scenario forced on him by Austrian tax collectors who were more than a little miffed by Tell's refusal to pay taxes.

As Lady Godiva and William Tell demonstrate, tax protests are nearly as old as taxes themselves. Taxes generate passion—feelings that can lead us to bitterness and unproductive behavior if they dominate our thinking. But channeled properly, passion about taxes can lead us to new heights of creativity.

40.

They Took Taxes Seriously

It's wise to keep the proper perspective on taxes, understanding that they're important without letting them dominate our lives. Yet there have been times when taxes were the principal issue in many lives—and with some justification. The great revolution that created the United States and the first serious threat to that union were fueled at least in part by tax policy. People feel passionate about taxes; to confirm that, just pick up any volume of American history.

One event in American history that was influenced by taxes occurred in the late eighteenth century, when the fledgling nation was strapped for cash and looking for any vehicle that could generate new revenue. In 1791, Congress enacted an excise tax on all distilled spirits. While large producers could accommodate the tax and still make profits, small distillers howled, claiming that the levy would drive them out of business.

Thus began what has come to be known as the Whiskey Rebellion. The Revolutionary War battle cry of "No taxation without representation" was fresh in the minds of the rebels; they took up their cause on several fronts. In western Pennsylvania, where the anti-tax fervor was white hot, rebels burned down the home of a tax collector and flirted with secession. Tax collectors elsewhere were tarred and feathered.

President George Washington called out the militia in 1794 to squelch the revolt. While many arrests were made, most of the suspects were acquitted for lack of evidence. Washington later pardoned all rebels who had been imprisoned but not yet tried or sentenced. The Whiskey Rebellion ran dry. It became little more than historical footnote, although some of the key western Pennsylvania sites in the drama are noted with markers today as points of historical interest.

It's important to remember that taxes typically play a supporting role in the drama of our lives; they usually don't get star billing. Yet there also may be those rare times when tax policy becomes something worth fighting about. Recognizing those historic occasions, and distinguishing them from less vital tax matters, will become easier for us as we become more conversant with the entire body of tax law and practices.

41.

A Different Look at
"Tax Freedom Day"

No one has to remind us of how long and how hard we must work to pay our bills—including our taxes. Lest we forget, the Tax Foundation each year gives us a precise measure of how many days we worked to meet our tax obligations.

In 2001, for example, the foundation announced that May 3 was "Tax Freedom Day," meaning that all the money that Americans earned from the start of the year through May 3—a total of 123 days—went for taxes. We worked fifty days to meet our income taxes, twenty-nine days to meet Social Security and Medicare taxes, and ten days to earn enough cash for property taxes.

The foundation, which spends more time studying this matter than it may be worth, also publishes a list of Tax Freedom Days by state; the exact day varies from state to state because of differing state taxes. According to the foundation, Connecticut has the heaviest tax burden in the land; the Constitution State's residents can't enjoy

Tax Freedom Day until May 25. By contrast, Alaskans may observe the holiday on April 16, the earliest celebration in the nation.

If your employer doesn't recognize Tax Freedom Day as an official holiday, don't look for it anytime soon. While the Tax Foundation issues a number of revealing studies each year and contributes valuable research, Tax Freedom Day adds little to the debate.

For one thing, it's one of those half-empty, half-full conundrums. If we accept the veracity of the foundation's research and agree that we work 123 days of the year to pay our taxes, does it not follow that we labor 242 days of each year absolutely tax-free? Trumpeting the fact that we're free of taxes two-thirds of the year doesn't seem to be part of anybody's mission.

Moreover, the concept of Tax Freedom Day omits an important part of the cost-benefit equation—the services that we get for our taxes. If our taxes are higher these days, it also may be true that our money is buying more and better government services. Our national security may be stronger, our highways better maintained, and our elected officials more accessible.

If our services *aren't* better while our taxes increase, we have every right to howl about it. Speaking out is one of the responsibilities of citizenship. But speaking out on taxes through such a limited vehicle as Tax Freedom Day doesn't tell the entire story.

42.

There's Life After Taxes

If we let them, taxes can dominate our lives. On a very few occasions, this may be justified. However, for most of us, most of the time, putting too much emphasis on taxes can be a serious mistake. That tunnel vision can keep us from being most effective in other areas of our lives and prevent us from enjoying the pleasures that invariably prove too fleeting. If you think that you can focus on taxes now to help you appreciate life later, you may have a case of misplaced priorities.

Whipping your tax attitude into shape and sharpening your tax-planning process are not ends in themselves. Rather, they're means to an end—financial stability and fulfillment for you and your family. We don't ever want to lose sight of the ultimate goals.

Taxes provide a wonderful base of support; a foundation for the lives that you want to build for you and your family. Concentrate on those lives. One of the great benefits of becoming tax-competent is that your new understanding and skills will free you from undue worry. There *is* life after taxes.

43.

Channel Your Passion into Planning

Taxes evoke passion. Why this is so isn't exactly clear. When our rates for water usage skyrocket, when we're required to pay more than last year to heat our homes or phone relatives across the country, we shrug, absorb the rate increases, and get on with life. But let taxes go up, and we're ready to storm the statehouse.

There's just something about taxes that affects us like no other financial obligation. The visibility of our legislators may contribute to our passion. You could try getting angry with your water authority, electric company, or telephone provider, but where would that lead you? Into a bureaucratic maze of countless phone calls, endless automated menus, and occasionally, a real-live human—who would cordially refer you to the next menu.

Legislators are high-profile. We know their names. Very often, they're our neighbors. If we call their offices, an aide will hear us out and pass along our complaints. We're familiar with their voting records because our daily newspaper prints them. Perhaps we're more passionate about taxes because we know that our fury will be felt, if not taken into account.

Such passion can be a good thing if properly channeled. If you get that urge to contact your legislator or local council member about a proposed tax law, do it. Act on your passion. Your representatives need to know the way that you feel.

After you've taken those steps, however, it's time to channel your passion into productive planning. The next time that you're ready to boil over about a tax hike, survey your tax team and ask them to explore additional areas for potential tax savings. (Calm down before you call them—they're on your side.) When you're gripped by a blinding rage over news that a cabinet nominee's nanny failed to pay federal income taxes, whip out last year's return and see how you're doing this year compared to last year.

With a little effort and creativity, you'll find useful ways to redirect your tax passion. Let the passion flow—into the right channels.

44.

How Expert Are the Experts?

Come tax time, everybody's a tax expert. If you don't believe it, just ask them. Through the months of January, February, and March, the ads sprout like weeds in every conceivable information garden. You see them in newspapers and magazines, and hear them on radio. They pop up in television newscasts and flutter as banners on the Internet. They all sound pretty much the same: "Free tax advice. No obligation! We guarantee the best results! You'll $ave big time with our $ervice! We'll be there with you for any audit! Guaranteed improvement over last year!"

Some ads go even beyond this, as the so-called experts solemnly pronounce that Americans overpay their taxes each year, and that incompetently prepared returns are the chief culprit. These gurus promise to review last year's returns, show you the error of your ways, and incorporate the new-and-improved approach into this year's preparations.

Enticing as they sound, you should view all of these ads as little more than unsubstantiated claims. It isn't that all such claims are necessarily exaggerated or untrue; it's that it's impossible to tell what parts of them are true.

If you do want to engage any of these "expert" consultants, you must be prepared to dedicate extensive research into their experience and expertise. Then you'll be better able to evaluate their claims.

Perhaps a better approach is to recruit the members of your tax team through recommendations from trusted friends and other word of mouth. Remember that the canons of ethics of some financial professions prohibit aggressive advertising. Even where it's ethically okay, many professionals regard advertising as unseemly and to be avoided at all costs. If you rely on advertising and its claims to lead you to your team members, you may never reach the people who are best positioned to help you.

Inflated tax advertisements prey on our fears that we are leaving money on the table with each tax return. With all the attention that you're now paying to your preparation, you no longer need to succumb to this fear, and you can evaluate tax advertising strictly on its merits.

45.

When No Advice is the Best Advice

People shy away from discussions about religion and politics, now more than ever in our politically correct age. Few folks, however, have the same reservations about taxes. Mention that you spent part of last evening working on your taxes, and the chances are good that you'll evoke a lively, office-wide discussion. It makes sense, doesn't it? Everyone must file taxes; it's the one thing in America that approaches a universal experience, a communal activity— something like listening to a radio show on a Sunday night was for an earlier generation.

The problem with these discussions is that if you really pay attention, you may find the din of advice and surefire solutions to be confusing at best, and harmful at worst. While everyone's tax situation bears some similarities to yours, everyone's circumstances are different than yours—and in key regards—as well.

Thus a colleague's plan to increase charitable contributions will make no sense for you if you're not itemizing your deductions. A buddy's decision to establish and claim an office in his home can be dangerous for you—particularly if you already have an office provided by your employer. Your sister-in-law's move to file for an extension this year could be disastrous if you follow suit, preventing you from completing the process within the time that you've set for the task and diminishing the sense of achievement that on-time completion can bring.

By all means, participate in these discussions. They enhance your camaraderie with your colleagues and family, and you never know when you might pick up something interesting or useful, such as the name of a financial professional who might be a candidate for membership on your team. But when thinking about adapting others' decisions to your own tax preparations, caution is the watchword.

Through your diligence and determination, you've become your own best tax advisor. You have the best insight into your own situation, and you're more capable than ever of making the best choices. More often than not, the best tax advice given by friends and family is no tax advice.

46.

Down on Commiseration Corner

You see it gathering often—at the water fountain, in the cafeteria, leaning on their cars in the parking lot before leaving work. It's "Commiseration Corner," the group of usual suspects who join forces to grouse about the local sports team, the latest company directive, or if you catch them on a sunny April morning, their taxes.

Perhaps you were once part of this group, but with your new expertise, your powerful tax team, and your confident attitude about taxes, Commiseration Corner doesn't seem the right place for you anymore, does it? The problem with this type of pity party is that it tends to be destructive rather than constructive. Sure, misery loves company. But at Commiseration Corner, bad habits and counterproductive attitudes are reinforced. If everybody else is having tax problems, then your own tax worries are nothing more than normal and don't need to be addressed.

It's not necessary to give Commiseration Corner a wide berth. These are your friends; go ahead and join them. But when it's your turn to step up to the podium, don't denigrate your achievements just for your colleagues' acceptance. Tell your friends what you've achieved. Do it with pride.

You don't have to delve too deeply into the details. Many of your buddies will tune you out once they hear how different and successful your approach is. The wisest of them, though, will pin you down later for your advice. When they do, pass along advice on your tax planning process without getting into the specifics of your return. You can serve as a model for tax planning to the folks down at Commiseration Corner.

47.

Be Proud, Not Envious

Has this ever happened to you? There's a town-wide real estate assessment, and your taxes are going up while your friend's are going down! You feel angry. The injustice of it all!

This is small-time thinking. As we've seen, the Tax Code includes thousands of breaks for certain groups—including you, if you're willing to look with a dispassionate eye. It would be impossible to style every tax break for every taxpayer, so why waste emotional time and resources on the advantages that other people may enjoy?

There's an even more important point here. In most cases, your friend is paying less in taxes than you because he or she is in a situation of less value than you. Is that what you really want—to lower your net worth so that you can achieve a lower tax bracket?

Of course, you want your tax team to help you take advantage of all of the tax breaks coming to you. But your overall objectives are success and fulfillment for you and your family. When you achieve those goals, be proud, rather than envious of others less successful than you.

48.

The Tax Code and You

No less an authority than Paul O'Neill, treasury secretary in the administration of President George W. Bush, took a critical look at the U.S. Tax Code. Here, in part, is O'Neill's review: "Our Tax Code is an abomination. Everyone who has anything to do with the Tax Code agrees it is just an unbelievable mess." Further, O'Neill said, the Treasury Department was determined to implement a simplification initiative.

O'Neill hardly was the first high-ranking public official to take on the Tax Code. Do taxes seem any simpler to you as a result? Probably not. The problem lies not with the intentions of any of the would-be simplifiers, be they congresspeople, administration officials, taxpayer organizations, or individual citizens on a mission.

Rather, the most vexing problem with Tax Code modification is that the tax game is what might be thought of as "zero sum." The rules—both specifically and in their overall impact—come complete with decided advantages and disadvantages. Tweak one rule and you may inadvertently affect five others and upset the delicate balance in our tax laws.

For example, if we cut corporate taxes to induce companies to locate in our communities, won't individual taxpayers have to make up for the lost revenue? If we create a tax deal so sweet for homeowners that everybody rushes out and buys a house, what happens to the rental industry—and all of the folks who've invested in multiunit rental buildings? The zero sum game is a tough one for everybody to win. Tax simplification is anything but simple.

The best way to approach the Tax Code—all 1.4 million words of it—is to familiarize yourself with the provisions that apply to you now. You don't have to get every nuance, but it is helpful to know where you and your team can get any information that you may need. As your circumstances change, you can tap those same sources for provisions that newly apply to you.

49.

Broaden Your
Understanding of Taxes

It's a given that you can't know everything about taxes, but it doesn't follow that you should be content with knowing nothing. You may not need or want an accountant's thorough knowledge of tax laws, but if you can broaden your understanding of taxes, you'll be able to make informed choices and feel more like an effective player in your own tax drama. As we all know, a feeling of competence helps create confidence, which in turn contributes to greater competence.

If you make the effort, you'll find many means of enhancing your tax knowledge. Reading tax-related articles in daily newspapers can keep you well informed. Many newspapers feature special tax coverage in the first quarter of each year designed to familiarize us with any changes in federal, state, and local tax laws that were finalized the previous year. These are worth your study—and you don't have to commit them to memory. Clip the articles that are most relevant to you and save them in a media file. You'll have them for handy reference as you continue your preparations.

Pay similar attention to radio and TV shows about taxes. In many communities, accountants and financial advisors sponsor radio and TV shows that offer tax information. Many such professionals find that advertising their services is of limited value to them, so they opt instead for "infomercials" as a way of publicizing their services. That may be their primary objective, but they still can be useful informational vehicles for you.

Local libraries and civic groups frequently offer tax seminars; as with newspaper features, these usually occur in the first quarter of the year, when the April 15 submission deadline looms large in all of our minds. Seminars provide you with the opportunity to ask questions about the particulars of your situation—something that newspaper articles or television programs sometimes can't offer.

Finally, most taxing bodies produce pamphlets about various aspects of taxes. These usually are free of charge and easy to read and grasp. Get as many of these as you can, and preserve them in your media file. Even those that don't appear relevant to you today might become more germane as your circumstances change over the years.

50.

Make Yourself Scam-Proof

With taxes as complex as they are, perhaps it's not surprising that many taxpayers find themselves vulnerable to scam artists. What is surprising is how many people fall prey to such rip-offs.

Among the most enduring of the phony tax schemes are what the IRS calls "abusive trust schemes." In these, what can begin as a legitimate trust becomes the foundation for layer upon layer of beneficiaries. Each time a distribution is made, heavy expenses are claimed as deductions, significantly reducing the tax liability. Some promoters charge five thousand dollars or more to create the bogus trust structure.

The problem in an abusive trust is that the original beneficiary or beneficiary group doesn't change, meaning that the whole structure is a fraud, designed to create the appearance of expenses that haven't actually been incurred. This ruse is so common that the IRS has identified two strains—the domestic version and the foreign variation. In 2001, to cite only one year, forty-five people were convicted in abusive trust scams; more than eighty percent of them received prison time.

Even more worrisome—and more widespread—is the "slavery reparation scam." In this one, hucksters advise African Americans that as descendants of slaves, they are entitled to reparations under a special act of Congress. There is no such law, of course, but that doesn't stop promoters from charging several hundred dollars to enroll naive taxpayers. (During the Reconstruction era, Congress actually did approve payment of forty acres and a mule as reparation to former slaves, but the bill was vetoed by President Andrew Johnson.) In 2001, the IRS received nearly 80,000 tax returns claiming more than $2.7 billion in slavery reparation refunds.

Given the complexity of tax law and its tendency to change, it se ems likely that scams are inevitable; but there's no reason why they should claim you as a victim. With the base of knowledge that you're building about taxes, you'll be able to recognize "too-good-to-be-true" schemes when you see them—yet another benefit of your new attitude about taxes.

51.

Don't Snub the Stub!

Knowing where you are in a given year—how much you've earned, how much you've already paid in taxes via income withholding—can be a key aid to your tax planning. One of the best ways to get a good feel for your tax standing is to study your pay stub. Most of us are interested primarily in the meat-and-potatoes portion of our pay package—the check, of course—but don't snub the stub! Read it thoroughly before you add it to your tax files.

The stub will help you project both your earnings and taxes for the year. For example, if you analyze your stub for the last pay period in March—the final payment in the year's first quarter—you can multiply your year-to-date earnings and tax payments by four to get a projected total for the entire year. This will help you determine if your withholding will cover your entire obligation, or if you should initiate an accrual program to help make up the shortfall.

Work through this process for your federal, state, and local taxes. Your year-to-date withholding will be itemized on each stub for each of those categories.

You may think that you know precisely what your annual income will be; it may even be embodied in a written agreement between you and your employer. But wages can be affected by many things. Overtime pay, bonuses, dockings, mandatory wage freezes—all of these can mean that you'll earn somewhat more or less than your work agreement specifies. Going through this exercise gives you real figures to work with, rather than projections.

You'll realize several other benefits, as well. If you're a part-time worker or contract employee and you still receive a pay stub, you'll find several categories of withheld pay that may serve as tax deductions for you. These could include health insurance and union dues.

At the very least, reviewing each pay stub will help you determine that you're being paid the correct amount, and that your employer is withholding your income for taxes as you've directed. That alone is worth the few minutes spent reviewing your stubs.

52.

You Can't Know Everything

You *can't* know everything about taxes. The Tax Code is 1.4 million words long, and it's always in flux. No other body of law is as dynamic as the tax code. In one recent year, Congress initiated more than 400 changes to the Tax Code. Even if you could somehow memorize the whole code, how could you ever keep up with changes when they pour in at the rate of 400 or so per year? And these changes don't include those at the state and local level, which aggravate the complexity of the task.

Even accountants, probably the most knowledgeable professional group in the tax arena, don't trust to memory, and they don't despair when they find that they can't know everything. Instead, they file information. They read bulletins and pamphlets from the IRS and other tax sources. They take courses. They earn professional education credits, enhancing and updating their familiarity with tax law.

If accountants can be comfortable with gaps in their tax knowledge, so can you. When you learn something new about taxes, don't kick yourself about not having known it previously. Instead, document the new data and preserve it in your files.

Rather than attempting to know everything, research where you can *find* everything that you may need. Keep all of your tax resources handy. This includes all of the contact numbers and e-mail addresses for your tax team so that you can reach them at a moment's notice. It should include contact numbers for all appropriate taxing bodies and web sites that you've found especially helpful for tax information.

Remember when our teachers told us that learning how to learn might be more important than any specific information that they could impart? We probably didn't appreciate it then, but we were the beneficiaries of a piece of wisdom that can help our tax planning and attitude.

53.

Pay Attention to Your Mail

The U.S. Tax Code is an intimidating document. Not the least frightening aspect of it is its changeability; at least some of the provisions are modified every year by Congress, so keeping up with the Tax Code is a tough job for even the most experienced professionals.

Don't worry about that. You've assembled a powerhouse team—they'll keep up with the Tax Code and its impact on you. There are many ways that you can contribute to the team effort that are less arduous than grasping the intricacies of the Tax Code. Perhaps the most simple of these is opening your mail.

Much of the tax-related information and documentation that you need will come to you via postal mail. For starters, most governments now mail out tax-return forms, including directions for electronic filing. While it isn't a big deal if you lose or accidentally pitch blank tax forms—they're easily replaceable—having them readily available gets you off to a timely start.

Sometimes, you'll receive forms that you never expected. If you earned money in a community that taxes visiting workers, you may get a tax form from that community. You may overlook this type of tax completely if you don't open your mail.

If you work for multiple employers or clients, typically they'll mail you official reports of earnings for any given year by January 31 of the following year. If you pay real estate taxes to local taxing bodies, such as municipalities and school districts, you'll likely be notified of your obligation by mail. Changes in the local tax rates also will be provided to you by mail. If the assessed value of your property changes, so will your tax bill. Notifications of assessment changes, too, are typically mailed out to taxpayers. Of course, if you've been selected for an audit, you'll be notified of that by mail. Pay attention. The last thing that you want to do is miss your hearing.

Not all tax-related mail is bad news. Many taxing bodies have instituted breaks for certain groups. For example, your city or state may provide tax relief for senior citizens or first-time homebuyers, to name only two possible categories. Application forms for these benefits most often are sent by mail, so if you ignore these packages, you can't apply for the tax breaks.

If your mail looks like it's from the government, open it and review it at once. If it's tax information, file it appropriately, and consult with your tax team if you need advice. As they say in the direct mail business, if you pay attention to your mail—you may already have won!

54.

The Mysteries of Brackets Revealed

Many people regard the phrase "tax bracket" with awe, as if taxes were a secret society and "tax bracket" was the phrase that allowed you in. There's nothing mysterious or sacred about brackets—they change all the time—but we seem to worry inordinately about them.

Brackets are nothing more than the income categories to which tax rates apply. There are brackets for federal income taxes, and most states have brackets, as well, although as we've seen, some states feature a flat income tax rate for all taxpayers.

At the federal level, the rates are graduated. For 2001, there were five brackets and corresponding rates, ranging from a low of 15 percent to a top rate of 39.1 percent. Some of the confusion about brackets stems from the practice of applying several tax rates simultaneously to the same taxpayer.

For instance, if you're a single filer and earned between $27,050 and $65,550 in 2001, part of your income was taxed at the lowest rate, part of it at the next rate up the scale. If you earn enough money, you actually may have all the rates applied to various portions of your income. Don't worry about this. It's essentially a math exercise that your tax team can handle.

More worrisome is the fear of some people that job promotions and other career successes should be avoided because the additional income will kick them into higher brackets. "Bracket inflation," they call it, or "bracket creep." It's certainly true that if your income advances past certain thresholds, part of it will be subject to taxes at a higher rate. But is this really something to fear or avoid?

Even if you pay more in taxes on your greater income, you still get to keep the biggest chunk of it. And you're not slave to a small-time, defeatist attitude that might lead you to accept less than what you could achieve. Achieve as much as you can, be the most successful person that you can be, and don't look at the world through bracket blinkers.

55.

How Many Exemptions?

Most of us became acquainted with the term "exemptions" when we opened our orientation packages at our first jobs or new jobs. Typically, we find a form asking how many exemptions we want to claim so that our employers can withhold a commensurate amount from our wages.

Exemptions are a mechanism that the government uses to remove part of your income from income tax liability. You get an exemption for yourself, your spouse, and any dependent children living with you. It's a way of softening the financial blow of raising a family, one of many provisions in the Tax Code that skews toward families. Exemptions are about the closest thing to "free money" that most of us will ever see, and their impact can be broader still.

For example, if you're supporting children from a previous marriage, these may qualify as exemptions. The same is true if you are supporting your aging parents. Both of these phenomena have become fairly common in the Baby Boom generation, yet some taxpayers may not be fully aware of the tax opportunities available. Make certain that you qualify; your preparer should be able to tell you whether or not you do.

Study those opportunities—and the income limitations, as well. The benefits do phase out at certain income levels. Married couples filing jointly are more likely to reach the income ceiling than individual filers, because the earnings limit for joint filers is less than double that of individual filers.

So when you fill out that tax form at work, remember that the number of exemptions that you claim will affect the amount withheld from your paycheck. The rough rule of thumb here: The more exemptions you claim, the less money will be withheld from your paycheck on the theory that your exemptions ultimately will result in a smaller overall tax obligation. But again, your claimed exemptions must be legitimate.

While you want to understand this area and the implications for your taxes, don't spend too much time worrying about exemptions. Check in with your tax team to make sure that they know all of the details about your dependents, and they'll likely be correct with your exemptions. It is a simple tax matter to ultimately revise your exemption information at work

56.

Taxes and Your Home

For most of us, the purchase of our homes will be the largest, most important acquisition that we ever make. As such, we devote considerable time to the selection, reviewing communities where we and our families are most likely to thrive, checking out schools and amenities, settling on just the right dwelling where we'll feel most comfortable—and which we can afford.

Many people make taxes part of their housing deliberations, as well. This is a good idea—if only because you'll get a sense of what real estate taxes will cost you. Many homeowners have their taxes and homeowners' insurance payments bundled right in with their mortgages. Unless they pay close attention, they're unsure how much of their monthly payment is for taxes.

It makes some sense to study the real estate levies in the communities that you're considering. In many communities, you'll be hit with multiple real estate taxes as soon as you become a property owner. These include taxes from the state, the county, the municipality, and the school district—in any combination. If you study the combined real estate taxes in each of your candidate communities, you'll be able to compare the totals and get a sense of the most agreeable community for tax purposes.

But how much weight should you give that advantage? There are many things to consider in selecting a home. If you have kids, the quality of the local schools is important, perhaps even the dealbreaker in your decision. Your education priorities will probably outweigh any tax advantage that you may realize elsewhere.

You'll be considering many other points, as well. Would your new residence provide convenient access to public transportation? Would your investment in this home be likely to appreciate—that is, could you sell your house at a profit? Would your home need significant repairs? Again, every one of these questions probably outweighs tax concerns.

As with all other aspects of tax planning, when you're purchasing a home, look at the big picture. Consider the tax implications, but buy the home that works best for you. You'll get more happiness from a well-chosen home than you would from any increment that you'd save on property taxes.

57.

After the Mortgage Is Paid

Few occasions in your life are more joyous than your final mortgage payment. You've done it! You've taken on the responsibilities of homeownership, made your nut each month even when you had to scratch and claw to do it, and you now have a house that's yours, free and clear. In a week or two, the deed will arrive from the bank, confirming the good work that you've accomplished.

This is cause for celebration, so the last thing in the world that you want is another piece of mail a few months down the road telling you that your homeowners' insurance policy has been canceled, or that you're delinquent in your local property taxes. Yet that could happen if you don't take care.

The problem, of course, is that many lending institutions pay local property taxes and insurance premiums for you. They don't actually underwrite these costs for you—they're not that generous. But they typically forward your payments to the appropriate insurers and taxing bodies, drawing on money that you send them with your monthly mortgage payments.

If there are changes in the local tax rates or your insurance premiums, the bank continues to make the payments, but you'll soon get a notice of a commensurate increase in your monthly mortgage package.

When you pay off your mortgage, the bank exits the equation, no longer making tax and insurance payments for you. These now become your responsibility. You could ignore the tax notices before, knowing that the bank would handle it. Now you are responsible for the payments.

Your insurance payments are even more urgent. Your insurer typically won't know to redirect the bills to you, and you'll risk cancellation if premiums aren't paid. Even as you're celebrating that last mortgage payment, it's a great idea to call your insurer and have future bills sent to you.

If you use a spending budget, be sure to add line items for property taxes and home insurance, even as you erase the line for mortgage. Remember, also, that your property taxes could change as the taxing bodies modify the applicable rates.

58.

The Advantages of Credit Card Debt

There was a time when the Tax Code encouraged credit card debt. There were no provisions that specifically rewarded consumers for purchasing by plastic, but they were allowed to deduct a portion of credit card interest.

Such provisions have been phased out—we can only speculate why. It could be that as the volume of credit card debt grew, our government was concerned about the adverse impact that would have on federal revenues. Or it could be that times were so flush that the government believed that it no longer needed to prime the consumer spending pump.

The upshot is that credit card debt no longer brings any tax advantages. You can't deduct any of it, and you can't use it to offset passive gains. So the logical question is: Why carry credit card debt at all?

This is not to say that some debt isn't appropriate—even advisable at times. We know that businesses must incur debt to launch and expand; they hardly could be expected to underwrite costly ventures with only the cash that they might have on hand. The same is true of the major purchases in your life. Few of us would have the cash to pay up front for the entire cost of a new home.

But there's a key difference with a mortgage loan. Your interest expenses are tax-deductible, as are certain costs for home improvements. With credit card debt, you get no similar advantages. You realize all of the disadvantages of debt and none of the tax advantages.

It follows, then, that rational management of your credit card debt load should be an important component of your tax planning. Avoiding excessive credit card debt won't bring you any direct tax gains, but you'll save money on interest payments, and you can earmark those funds for investments that *will* make a tax difference. Think of it as the "fantastic plastic" approach.

59.

Those Are the Breaks

Rather than being a pleasant, cultivated garden, our tax laws are a riotous patch that appears to have sprouted like weeds. This year may bring breaks for farmers. Next year, farmers may be forgotten in favor of the fishing industry. The following year, some other industry may weigh in with enough lobbying muscle to win its share of breaks.

All of this tends to give our body of tax laws a haphazard and temporary feeling, and it would be hard to deny that charge. Yet our tax laws do seem to embody breaks that reflect some of our values as a society; specific provisions may change over the years, but these emphases remain the same.

An obvious set of breaks would be those related to child-rearing. Your children become exemptions right from the start, and the breaks continue thereafter. You may itemize and deduct certain childcare costs, and you'll enjoy deductions for your children's education, as well. This thrust of the Tax Code is in keeping with our belief in families and family values.

Homeownership, too, is a cherished part of the American Dream, so those who purchase homes also get breaks on their taxes. Interest on mortgage loans usually can be deducted, as can interest for home-equity loans. Improvements that increase the value of your home fall into the same category. Proceeds from the sale of your home also can be deductible in certain cases.

When you hear people rail against tax breaks, they may have some justification. Sometimes, tax breaks do appear to be little more than ploys to assist the already overprivileged. Yet it's also wise to remember that breaks are extended to many large, deserving groups of taxpayers. If you're not a member of any of these groups now, chances are that you will be someday, and that you will be enjoying tax breaks.

It is odd to think that the things we value as a society are reinforced haphazardly, through our Tax Code. Maybe there's some method to the madness, after all.

60.

Gimme Shelter

You may have heard people boasting about tax shelters that they've discovered, perhaps triggering feelings of envy in you. Even though you weren't entirely sure what a tax shelter was, you wanted a piece of the action. Relax. You weren't necessarily missing out on any great benefit.

A tax shelter is generally defined as an investment that can reduce current tax liability by creating losses that offset income from other areas. Say you invest in racehorses, an almost surefire losing investment, as any horseman or horsewoman will tell you. You can use your horse ownership losses to offset income from other sources. You have a lot of fun following your horses, and because of the offset, you lose a lot less than it might seem.

The problem here is that this approach can be in conflict with IRS rules. The government considers as "abusive shelters" those investments that are designed to do little more than lose money. If you invest in a tax shelter, the IRS may want to question you about the real intent of your investment, and it may ask you to produce specific documentation of the expenses that you claim.

In the case of our example of horse ownership, the IRS has gone even further, establishing a sort of test—how many hours per week you spend on your horses—to determine if it's a business or a hobby. If the government determines that it's the latter, your shelter could be reduced to rubble and your taxes will be restated. Use an abusive shelter, and you could be penalized up to a thousand dollars to boot.

It isn't that legitimate shelters can't be helpful; even the IRS recognizes the validity of some. The biggest problem with shelters is that in focusing on them, you spend too much of your time and effort trying to "game" the IRS and deflect attention from your real focus—becoming a business success and a self-fulfilled human being. Concentrate on those goals. If you make enough money, your taxes will take care of themselves.

61.

When to Itemize

If you've been accepting the standard deduction offered to you by the federal government as a way of simplifying your taxes, now is the perfect time to consider itemized deductions. You may have been avoiding these because you feared the added burden of document collection and preservation. Perhaps you weren't sure of exactly what's involved in itemization. But with your new tax attitude and expertise, you can overcome that fear of filing and be ready to tackle itemization.

First, let's clarify what is meant by itemization. It's a line-item listing of certain expenses and losses specified by the government as offsets to your income. If you operate a business, you're already itemizing your business expenses and losses. For many, doing the same with personal expenses and losses will make equal sense.

You can itemize quite a few categories of expenses and losses. Unreimbursed expenses for medical and dental care can be itemized, for example, if the total exceeds 7.5 percent of your adjusted gross income. Most of the local taxes that you pay in any year can be itemized on your federal taxes as offsets to your income. Home mortgage interest, as well as interest paid on home equity loans, can be itemized, but credit card interest is not eligible.

Charitable contributions can be itemized, as can certain gambling losses. You can offset any winnings from gambling, such as money won through the lottery, if you can document an equal amount in losses. But the amount that you claim in losses can't exceed your winnings.

Documentation is especially important when you itemize. If you donate clothes to a local charitable organization, for example, make sure that you get a receipt that specifies the value of your contribution, and save the receipt in your tax files. The rules on itemization are thick, so you may want to solicit advice from your tax team on the eligibility of certain expenses.

However, your determination on the advisability of itemization is not difficult. Do rough calculations of your total projected itemizations for the year, and then compare them to the standard deduction. If your total itemizations would be higher, that's the way to go.

62.

Are You Withholding Properly?

For most of us, having our employers withhold part of our wages each payday is as natural a part of the job as performance reviews and coffee breaks. Yet withholding is a relatively recent addition to our tax protocol, having been adopted by Congress only in 1943. Now, it would be hard to imagine the tax collection process without it.

It seems a fairly simple matter. You receive that new employee package your first day on the job, you find the withholding form, you declare the number of exemptions, and that's that. Yet there are some subtle matters here for your consideration as an efficient tax planner. The dangers are withholding too little and withholding too much.

Many taxpayers like to have more withheld from their pay than they ever would need to fulfill their tax obligations. Their reasoning is that the bite from their paychecks is relatively light, and they'll be delighted to get that refund after April 15.

If this sounds like you, think of what you're actually doing. Since the IRS doesn't provide interest on overpayments, you're putting your money into a bank account of sorts that isn't paying you anything for the privilege. You'll get your refund, but your money will have lost buying power while it was resting in that interest-free account.

A better approach might be to adjust your withholding downward and earmark the increment that you receive each payday for savings or investing. You'll probably end up substantially ahead of where that refund would get you.

The other danger—withholding too little—has more obvious consequences: You face a potentially heavy payment come April 15. If you find that this is the case, adjusting your withholding upward is the simple fix.

The moral to this tale is that you must pay attention to that thick packet of orientation documents that you get from your employer. Some of the documents will have tax implications that will be simple enough if you address them promptly. If you change employers, you'll want to pay even more attention to getting your withholding right.

63.

All Hail Cottage Industries!

In 1997, the number of self-employed Americans surpassed the ten million mark. That number represented an all-time high that will be eclipsed before long because self-employment is a growing trend. Millions of Americans are taking charge of their lives and careers as they pursue their own unique visions for the future.

As the newly self-employed have networked with each other to form potent alliances, pundits have coined a term to describe this phenomenon—"cottage industries." The sobriquet may not do this new structure justice. Alliances of the self-employed are a powerful and growing force in the American economy.

When you strike out on your own, you have many priorities to consider. Will you work in your home? What sort of communications network will you need, and where will you find the cash to finance it? How about a new identity package—business cards, logo, letterhead stationery, and the like? Would a web site help you, and can you afford to design and maintain one?

One of the last things that you want to worry about is the impact of your professional transformation on your taxes, but you need to prioritize that as quickly as possible. How you structure your business can have profound implications on your taxes. You'll have a number of options here, ranging from corporation to sole proprietorship to partnership (if others are involved with you). Even within these broad categories, there are additional options. Your choice here will have a number of major tax consequences; you'll want to review these with your tax team well before you make the jump.

Remember also that when you're self-employed, no employer is withholding a portion of your income for taxes. You're entirely responsible for your tax obligations now—and you probably must begin filing estimated taxes each quarter, no matter how you've structured your business. You'll need to provide earnings reports to any consultants that you may hire, and if you add a few full-time employees, you'll have to withhold a portion of *their* income for taxes. You'll also get up-close and personal with the self-employment tax, which covers Social Security and Medicare taxes.

When you're self-employed, itemization of your legitimate business expenses becomes almost mandatory. You'll need those deductions to thrive in your new circumstances.

Self-employment has tax implications that can't be overlooked. As with all aspects of taxes, don't let these become the driving force in your business decisions. Taxes are one aspect of your new career that must be addressed, but no more than that.

64.

When Deferral Is a Good Thing

Deferral" is one of those words that has evolved to cover a multitude of sins. When we say that we'll defer action on something today, that usually means that it's an unpleasant or arduous task that we'll get around to at some unspecified time in the future—and only if forced to. When it's done in a legislative arena, deferral is a way of killing bills that have no chance of passage, without forcing anyone to record a "no" vote that could antagonize the constituents back home.

When it comes to taxes, however, deferral is a good thing. In this context, deferral means that the taxes you ordinarily would pay on certain categories of income are deferred until far into the future. The obligation to pay taxes on this income still exists, but you don't have to honor your obligation now. The theory is that by the time the taxes come due, you'll be earning less overall—you might even be retired and out of the workforce—and your tax bracket will be lower. Therefore, your taxes on deferred income will be less than they would be now, when you may be at the height of your earning power.

A number of investment opportunities offer deferred taxes as an attractive incentive. These include most types of Individual Retirement Accounts (IRAs) and the 401(k) plans offered by many employers. When considering these categories of savings plans, you'll always want to review any tax-deferral features. For example, do the plans require distributions at a certain age? That's something that you'll need to know, because that's when your taxes will kick in.

Also remember that deferral privileges typically apply to federal income taxes, but in some cases cannot be extended to state and local taxes. You and your tax team should get a handle on the applicable laws where you live.

While you're actively seeking out deferral opportunities, don't apply the same concept to your tax planning and preparation. Adhere to your schedule as much as possible. Deferral may be a good thing where investments are concerned, but in the area of tax preparation, it seldom is.

65.

Are Estimated Payments for You?

The growing phenomenon of self-employment in America poses an unusual tax collection challenge for the federal government. When virtually all of us were paying the bulk of our tax obligations through salary withholding, the IRS could count on collecting the biggest portion of our taxes virtually automatically. But with the self-employed wholly responsible for their taxes without the aid of withholding, how can the government assure collection?

The answer is the estimated tax. Generally, if your projected federal income tax obligation for the year exceeds one thousand dollars and you're not meeting that obligation through withholding, you're responsible for estimating your taxes and paying one-fourth of the amount each quarter.

Estimated taxes are a movable feast. If your income for the year exceeds your projection, your estimated payments for the following year will be based on this year's actual income, so they'll increase. It's the same principle if you earn less than your projected income—your estimated payments will decline the following year.

Estimated payments are required of corporations, as well as other business entities, so you probably need to consider them regardless of your business structure. Unemployment compensation, lump sum distributions, and still other forms of income can be subject to estimated payments.

Once you determine that your income is subject to estimated taxes, the process is fairly straightforward. You'll need to file separate forms and submit separate payments each quarter, rather than lumping estimated payments in with your annual tax return. Underpaying your estimated taxes can subject you to penalties and interest. Under current law, your total estimated payments for this year must equal one hundred percent of last year's taxes, or ninety percent of the current year's actual obligation, whichever is smaller.

One way to avoid the penalty is to make an ad hoc adjustment to your estimated payments. For example, suppose that in the year's third quarter, you land a big contract that will vault you above your projected earnings for that year. In that case, add a little extra to your estimated payments for the third and fourth quarters. If the IRS objects to receiving that extra money, it will be the first time!

Don't think of estimated taxes as a burden. Rather, think of them as a handy control mechanism that keeps you firmly on the tax track—and helps you avoid an unpleasant surprise when you file your annual return.

66.

If You Relocate...

One of the distinguishing characteristics of most progressive societies is the mobility of its citizens. When people were tied to the land or a job, the tax collector knew where to find them and how to assess them. Now, we have the wherewithal and transportation to move around at will—and the communications systems to keep us in touch, wherever we may land.

In America's so-called New Economy, changing jobs and locales regularly is perceived as an indication of upward mobility. The technology-driven economy will bubble up new hotspots periodically, this theory goes, and you must seek out those geysers to stay hot yourself. It stands to reason, then, that our mobility can make our tax situations a little more complex.

Your relocation is not much of a problem for the federal government, as long as your return always lists your current address. The challenges that you encounter may lie instead with your state and local taxes. The rates and even the structure of your taxes may vary significantly as you move through various jurisdictions.

For example, let's say that you live in Pennsylvania for five months of a given year but reside the balance of the year in Hawaii. Pennsylvania's income tax is a straightforward 2.8 percent, no matter your income, but Hawaii has nine different income tax brackets. Determining your bracket will be one part of the task. Then you'll need to file in Pennsylvania at the applicable rate for your five months there, and in Hawaii at the applicable rate for your seven months there. Your move will change the local levies, as well, and you'll need to file in every municipality in which you lived that year.

When you move, you'll have quite a portfolio of returns to file, but your tax team can probably handle them without any problems. More importantly, keep accurate records of your residential history, and don't worry too much about the arithmetic. If a move is attractive on its own merits, make it. You'll figure out the tax implications in due time.

67.

Changes in Status

As we've seen, relocation will probably affect your taxes. Other changes in key areas of your life could affect your tax situation, as well.

A change in your marital status will create obvious impact. If you go from single to married, or married to divorced, your filing status may change, as can the whole roster of taxes and deductions. Even if you stay married but change your filing status from "married filing jointly" to "married filing separately" (or the reverse), you'll have a revised set of tax issues to consider.

The situation becomes even more complex if your status changes midyear. Then you have one filing status for part of the year, and another for the balance of the year.

Changes in jobs can have an equally significant effect, particularly in the withholding area. If your new employer withholds part of your salary at a rate different than that of your former employer, you could end up with an inadvertent underpayment or overpayment. If you change municipalities or states along with your job, the situation becomes even more complicated.

Career shifts can have even more subtle implications. Imagine that you're self-employed with a home office for part of a given year, and then take a full-time job outside of your home for the balance of the year. You may have legitimate home-office deductions for that part of the year when you were self-employed, but can you continue to claim your home office when your employer is providing you with work quarters? Probably not.

As with relocation, status changes bring some math problems that your tax team can handle. Your role should be to keep accurate records of all of the major changes in your life, so that you can provide reliable information for the calculations. Always take the long view on status changes. Success and fulfillment for you and your family are your principal goals. Make choices that lead to those goals. You can handle the corresponding tax ramifications.

68.

Helping Others Helps Your Taxes

If we choose, we can look at the Tax Code as a series of technical provisions with little underlying philosophy. But as we've seen, our Tax Code works to promote homeownership and families, which are among the core values at the foundation of our society. Yet another basic thrust of the Tax Code is support for charitable organizations.

We help fully accredited charitable groups by donating money or goods to them; the government helps us help charities by allowing us to itemize our contributions and deduct them from our income for tax purposes. This encourages charitable contributions, thereby enhancing the "good works" in our communities.

Think of all of the charitable organizations at work where you live. Food pantries, places of worship, and animal shelters all contribute to our communities. Without the selflessness of these organizations, our cities and towns would be unlivable. How wonderful that our support for them provides direct financial benefits for us, as well.

Our network of charities is so strong and diverse that supporting them is a win-win situation. Yet there are a few measures that you should take as a matter of routine when supporting your favorite charities.

First, make sure that your beneficiaries have been certified as charities with tax-exempt status. Not all are. We're all familiar with ad hoc groups that spring up to help victims of a fire, say, or to finance a young athlete's Olympic training. These may be noble causes, and you may want to participate, but if these groups lack official status, you may not be able to deduct any contributions. That doesn't mean that you shouldn't donate, but you should know what you're getting into.

Also, document your contributions. Many charitable organizations have standard receipt books; they'll be happy to provide a receipt for you. If they don't, ask for a makeshift receipt. If a receipt is beyond their capabilities, donate by check; your canceled check can be your documentation.

Finally, if you want tax credit for donations in this calendar year, make your donations in this calendar year, as well. From the recipients' point of view, timing is probably not a vital issue. Your favorite charity will still need your contribution next year, and you'll still benefit from the deduction.

69.

Being Charitable—
In Good Years and Bad

As noted, the federal government allows us to itemize our deductions to certified charities, lowering our tax bills while providing life-giving support for some of our worthiest organizations. For those organizations, however, the tax aspects of donations are a mixed blessing.

When times are flush and most of us are awash in disposable income, we max out our charitable contributions; our beneficiaries come to count on that income, perhaps using it to expand current programs or underwrite new initiatives. Then times turn lean. When we find ourselves struggling to pay bills, about the last thing that we want to hear is that nonprofit groups still need our money. But if we turn off the spigot, all of those new and enhanced outreach programs may be imperiled.

Most of us ride an income roller coaster, so it's reasonable to expect that our charitable beneficiaries will endure the same dips and dives. But you can help regulate your contributions, if that's a goal of yours. Some people routinely "tithe," allocating ten percent of their income to their churches. Charitable giving can follow the same principle, though you may want to reduce the level.

Think of your contributions as a set percentage of your income—one percent is a figure that many taxpayers find comfortable. If you hit the jackpot one year and earn $100,000, your charitable contributions will total one percent of that—$1,000. If you scrape bottom the next year and earn only $30,000, your charitable gifts will total $300—still one percent of your income.

If you adopt a percentage for charitable gifts, you'll continue to help your community, but you'll do it at a level that's always within reach. There's nothing sacred about the one percent solution; if you're able to donate at a two percent or three percent rate, even better. But the one percent plan won't bankrupt you, you'll continue to garner deductions, and you'll remain a force for good.

70.

Taxes and Your Investments

Never before have so many people been investors. The explosion was fueled in part by the great technology boom of the late twentieth century, when high-flying Internet companies enriched thousands of employees and shareholders—all of them in need of attractive investment vehicles for their newfound wealth. For this group, a tame certificate of deposit or sleepy little savings account would hardly do.

Also a contributing factor was uncertainty about the solvency of the Social Security system. If workers weren't sure that Social Security would provide for them in their old age, then it followed that they would need to find other retirement savings plans in the private sector. This became a quest of some urgency for taxpayers at all income levels.

If you're exploring investment opportunities to help secure your future, as millions of others are, then you need to consider the tax consequences of your investments. Where investments are concerned, taxes are a double-edged sword. You need to know the tax implications of every potential investment, but you don't want to allow taxes to guide your decisions.

Some investment opportunities typically are described as "tax-free" or "tax-deferred," which may be true enough, as far as it goes. But does that description go far enough? For one thing, the touted tax benefits may not apply across the board. You may realize a break on your federal income taxes only to find that it doesn't apply to state and local taxes.

Perhaps more importantly, a tax break won't do you much good if your investment goes south. In that unhappy event, your investment won't generate any taxable income, and you could lose your principal in the deal.

That's why tax ramifications always must play no more than a supporting role in your investment decisions. Research all of the terms and conditions of the investments that you're considering. If stocks, bonds, or mutual funds are involved, get a good understanding of the underlying value of the companies or government entities issuing the stocks and bonds. Only when you have a feel for that core value are you ready to factor taxes into the mix. If you select solid investment vehicles that help your money grow, you won't be too unhappy about the corresponding taxes.

71.

Tax-Free Doesn't
Necessarily Mean "Free"

There's no such thing as a free lunch." That may be the signature wisdom of our era. It summarizes the hard truth that we've learned through years of experience—things that sound impossibly good usually come with a hidden price. It's a tough lesson to learn sometimes, but now that we know it, we should apply this philosophy to our tax preparation and planning. You can find investments that are tax-free, but there may be a price to pay.

Consider the investment category known as tax-free municipal bonds. Cities and counties issue these to underwrite a broad range of local improvements, hoping to sell bonds to taxpayers. They use our money and provide us with return on our investment that is tax-free. Sounds fine, and it is to a point.

But there's another type of municipal bond that looks the same as the tax-free vehicle in most ways. The difference is that our profits count as taxable income. Since the return on taxable bonds can be higher than that for their tax-free cousins, it sometimes makes sense to invest in the taxable variety and accept the tax burden—your profits still may be higher because of the better rate of return. In these cases, tax-free is free, but not necessarily better.

To determine which type of bond is better for you, you can plot out your return and factor in the prospective taxes. The point is not to involve you in a lot of calculations; rather, it is to suggest that you be as cautious about claims in the tax arena as you are in other aspects of your life.

When you're considering tax-free investments, involve your tax team in the deliberations. Let them run the numbers to confirm that tax-free vehicles are the way to go. If you rely on research, careful planning, and the advice of your team, you'll avoid excesses of both cynicism and gullibility.

72.

Don't Be Passive with Passive Income

As you diligently prepare the groundwork for your tax returns, you may encounter documents about assets and accounts that you were only vaguely aware of. A report arrives in the mail indicating that you earned dividends from stock holdings and a life insurance policy, neither of which you've thought about for the past year. There's a document advising that you earned several hundred dollars in savings from checking and passbook accounts and a certificate of deposit; you've been routinely filing these documents without paying attention to them.

For tax purposes, this type of revenue is called "passive income." Presumably, the government calls it "passive" because you weren't out there performing physical labor to earn it. This may be a misnomer—you were pretty active in earning the money to pay for these investments, and you had to make active decisions on acquiring them. Nevertheless, the government considers this type of income as indistinguishable from ordinary income, and taxable at the same rates.

If you've forgotten about some of these assets, the influx of passive income can make quite a difference in your tax obligation; an increase that you may be unprepared to pay. So it's time to get active with passive income.

First, gain a comprehensive understanding of all of the assets that could produce passive income. These would include securities, mutual funds, insurance policies, bank accounts, and CDs. Last year's tax return should give you a good handle on your passive income—not this year's income totals, necessarily, but the sources of that income.

Now, you're ready to consider taking some "passive losses" to offset your passive gains. For example, has a stock that you purchased some time ago declined in value, so that selling it now would create a loss? If you take that loss now, you'll offset some of your passive income.

Bring your tax team into these discussions, and ask them about the underlying value of the assets involved. You might not want to sell a promising stock that's temporarily stagnant just to offset a few hundred dollars in passive income. Develop an active game plan for passive income, but remember that your goal remains your long-term financial well-being.

73.

And Baby Makes Three

The trials and tribulations of raising a family can be described in many ways. Yet no matter the family, and no matter who's doing the describing, the word "expensive" is sure to crop up time and again. We like to think that as our children grow, the costs of providing for them will diminish. What happens instead is that cost categories change, but our outlay seldom gets any smaller.

Costs for formula and diapers end, but they're replaced by the need for school clothes and supplies. Just when our kids stop needing closets full of new clothes, we must begin thinking of college costs. And of course, the need for medical care is constant.

Our Tax Code believes in families, and it helps soften the expense of child-rearing. The laws don't actually state this commitment to families, but it's evident in a number of family-friendly provisions.

For starters, you can claim your baby as a dependent, adding a personal exemption to your roster. You're able to introduce this benefit in the calendar year of your child's birth, no matter when during the year that birth occurred. If your child joins the world on Christmas 2003, for example, you still realize the full year's benefit for 2003.

You're also eligible for a child tax credit for each child. The credit is set at six hundred dollars per child in 2002, but is scheduled to be increased incrementally to a thousand dollars per child by 2010. (As with all tax policy, the child tax credit is subject to amendment by Congress, so it's best to keep current with any changes. There are income limitations for the child credit, so not everyone will realize the full measure of the benefit.)

This benefit is structured as a credit, meaning that you get a dollar-for-dollar reduction in your tax bill. Say you owe a thousand dollars in federal income taxes. If you have one child, that six-hundred-dollar credit reduces your tax bill to four hundred dollars. In certain cases, you're even entitled to a refund if your tax bill is less than your total amount of child credits.

Another compelling feature of this provision is that certain costs related to adoption also can be credited against your tax bill. This credit is subject to income limitations, as well, but you can take comfort in the fact that at the heart of our government is a Tax Code with a conscience.

74.

Tax Credit for Childcare

O dd as it may seem, the quality of life for parents in our society is often determined by the availability and affordability of childcare. The problem is more severe than missing a night out because we can't find a babysitter. We all know of single parents who've been forced to decline job offers or promotions because their earnings would be offset by the costs of childcare.

In support of families, the Tax Code does offer a bit of help here through a tax credit for childcare. In many cases, you can receive a tax credit for some of your childcare costs based on your income. Certain preschool and kindergarten costs also may be eligible for the childcare credit. The credit diminishes at higher income levels but doesn't completely phase out, so that everyone can receive at least some tax credit for some childcare expenses.

Don't assume, however, that the credit is automatic. The government typically wants to know the name, address, and tax identification number of your childcare provider to verify that it's a legitimate, tax-paying business. For this reason, it's a good idea to get the pertinent information up front as you're interviewing childcare prospects. Are you working with tax-paying individuals or institutions, and do they conform to all licensing requirements? It's a good idea to know this before you claim the childcare credit.

Much as you may want the credit, it can pose a dilemma for you if your principal care providers are relatives, neighbors, or friends—none of them qualified childcare vendors. It's not uncommon for single moms to form a network of childcare providers—they tap each other for sitting services. But this type of arrangement usually won't qualify for childcare credit, either.

Should you abandon your current sitters in favor of professional providers whose services will generate the tax credit for you? Probably not. The most important attributes of childcare providers—they're responsible for the well-being of your kids, after all—are experience, reliability, and compatibility. If you have those qualities in the people who sit with your kids, stick with them. Valuable as it might be, the tax credit isn't worth as much as the peace of mind that your current sitters bring you.

75.

The Kiddie Tax

Children are invaluable assets. We devote our lives to nurturing and teaching them, and it turns out that we learn as much *from* them as we impart *to* them. They enrich our lives in countless ways.

For years, many parents tried to utilize their kids for literal enrichment. By placing a portion of their assets in the names of their children, parents hoped to avoid taxes on those assets. This was not the sort of enrichment that the government envisioned when it provided tax breaks for child-rearing, so it took steps to halt the practice.

The result was the so-called "kiddie tax," a Tax Code change imposed in 1986 to prevent such income-shielding. Simply stated, the law now provides for taxes on the income of your children. The concept is straightforward enough, but there are some nuances that you should understand.

The age of fourteen is a key watershed in the application of kiddie taxes. If your child is younger than fourteen, earned income up to the standard deduction is not taxed, while earned income greater than the standard deduction is taxed at the child's rate. Presumably, that rate is a lot lower than the rate on your own income.

As of summer 2002, for unearned income, such as interest and dividends, the first $750 is not taxed. Earnings between $750 and $1,500 are taxed at the child's rate, while earnings beyond $1,500 are taxed at your rate, unless your child's rate is higher.

A key change occurs at the age of fourteen; thereafter, unearned income greater than $750 is taxed at the child's rate. That's quite a benefit if your child's tax rate is lower than yours.

The kiddie tax can affect how you and your family structure some assets. For example, a savings account that will yield more than $1,500 in annual interest may make more sense after your child turns fourteen, when the income is taxed at the child's rate rather than yours. Keep current with earnings thresholds and other aspects of kiddie tax laws. As with all aspects of the Tax Code, they're not written in stone.

A final element in the mix concerns education aid. When they're mulling over financial-aid decisions, colleges consider assets in your child's name to be more readily available to help fund education costs than assets in your name. So significant holdings in your child's name could diminish the chances for financial aid, or reduce the amount of aid that's eventually offered. Even if college is a few years down the road for your kids, this is something to ponder now as you structure assets.

76.

Whose Asset Is It Anyway?

Creating assets in your children's names can be an attractive savings and tax-planning strategy. As we've seen, passive income earned by your kids in some cases is taxed at a lower rate than it would be had *you* earned it. So there are advantages, not the least of which is that this practice can enhance your children's self-esteem—they're participating in family finances now, an important new role for them.

But placing assets in the names of your youngsters can bring some interesting ethical dilemmas. What happens, for example, if after you establish a savings account for your child, you find that you need to tap that money for household emergencies? Is that something that you should do? Is it something that you *can* do? Technically, those assets now belong to your child and are unavailable to you.

Then again, if you decide to keep all of your assets in your name, mentally earmarking a portion of them for your kids' education, are you more likely to draw down that cash as needed? If you do, what happens when it's time to pay for tuition, and you've drained the accounts that presumably were reserved for education?

The real question here is about ownership of the asset. If it's in your child's name, it may be best to consider your child the owner of that asset and the asset off limits to you. That's consistent with the legal view, and it's probably the most ethical decision, as well.

If you adopt this approach, you must carefully consider the ramifications of establishing assets in your kids' names. When you go that route, a chunk of your own money becomes unavailable. You're not exactly giving it away—it stays within the family—but the impact on your immediate finances may be much the same. If you think that you may need that money down the road, keep it in your name.

It's great to give your kids hands-on financial experience. For you, a hands-off philosophy on your children's assets is best.

77.

Saving for College
Through Tax Planning

As you contemplate the future of your family, nothing may darken your day so much as the looming costs of college. By 2019, when today's toddler is ready for college, the four-year cost for a typical publicly supported college will be $162,326 (assuming annual tuition increases of six percent—the actual rate between 1997 and 2001). If your child opts for an elite, private school, the costs soar even higher.

While there's no way to sugarcoat this pill, the Tax Code endeavors to help parents in ways both large and small. One of the most interesting and useful outreach efforts to parents is through Section 529 of the Tax Code, which allows you to establish accounts targeted for education expenses—with corresponding tax breaks.

When you start a 529 plan, you can contribute up to $55,000 to your account ($110,000 for married couples) without triggering gift taxes, as long as you don't contribute any more for the next five years. You can continue making contributions until the account balance reaches $246,000; when funds are distributed to your child for qualified education purposes, your beneficiary pays no taxes on those funds. Everyone is eligible for a 529 account because there are no income limits.

Many states offer 529 plans; you can open an account in any state, regardless of where you live. However, plans may offer different features and investment philosophies, so a little research on your part is in order. You'll also want to check out prepaid tuition plans offered by many colleges and universities. While these typically don't bring the tax advantages of a 529 plan, they offer other features that you and your children might find attractive.

Your children's future may be paramount in your mind now, but don't forget about your continuing education. If you're thinking about going back to school, the Tax Code supports your dreams through two programs—the Hope Credit and the Lifetime Learning Credit.

The maximum credits and earnings limits have been in flux for these programs, so it's a good idea to check with your tax team or the IRS to get the most current figures. If you've been on the fence about returning to school to broaden your perspective or acquire new skills, remember: You may be rewarded with tax credits if you take the plunge.

78.

IRAs

An Individual Retirement Account, or IRA, can be a great investment for you, as long as you understand the tax implications. IRAs were created as an investment vehicle for the self-employed, who clearly could not participate in employer-sponsored savings plans. They've become so useful and so popular that now, even those with full-time jobs can open IRA accounts under certain circumstances.

The principal benefit of IRAs comes in the area of taxes. In some cases, the contributions that you make each year are tax-deductible; they're subtracted from your income that year, so you pay no taxes on those funds. Just as significant, as the balance in your account grows, you pay no taxes on those gains now. Depending on the type of IRA, either your account grows tax-free, or taxes are deferred until you begin taking distributions.

An equally compelling feature of IRAs is that you're in control. You determine what, if anything, you contribute in a given year. If you opt to max out your contribution, no one will tell you that you can't. If you choose to contribute nothing one year, that, too, is your option.

Even when we take the long view on taxes, we sometimes succumb to the feeling that tax breaks are for others, not for us. Any time that mood threatens to overtake you, remember the IRA. It's a tax break that's widely available, and it gives you an uncommon degree of flexibility and control. Now that you're taking control of your taxes, a vehicle that depends on your planning and decision-making should be empowering and enticing.

79.

But Which IRA?

IRAs present wonderful investment and tax-saving opportunities, and they optimize your control. That also means that you have the responsibility of selecting the right IRA for you, and this will require some thought.

IRAs have become so popular that the federal government has introduced several variations in recent years to broaden participation. There are three principal types of IRA—traditional IRAs, Roth IRAs and nondeductible IRAs—with differences both obvious and subtle.

In some cases, you won't have any choice about your IRA because the income limitations of the three types may dictate which version you choose. Beyond that, there's much to consider.

In a traditional IRA, for example, your contributions function as deductions—you pay no taxes on them—and the taxes on your account gains are deferred. In the Roth variation, your contributions are not tax-deductible, but there are no taxes at all on your account growth. Which is better for you? There's no set answer for that.

You'll have other variables to consider as well. With traditional and nondeductible IRAs, distributions are mandatory when you reach the age of seventy and a half. Roth IRAs require no distributions at any age; you can let your account grow as long as you please. With traditional IRAs, early withdrawals are taxed and assessed a ten percent penalty. (Certain exceptions are allowed.) With Roth IRAs, you may access your funds without penalty once they've been invested for five years and you're using the money for qualified purposes, such as higher education or medical expenses.

The maximum annual contribution to all three types has also been the subject of Congressional fine-tuning; the limit is scheduled to increase to five thousand dollars by 2008, when it will be indexed to inflation.

It will be helpful to get your tax team involved in researching and evaluating IRAs with you; at the very least, they'll provide you with the most current information on income and contribution limits and any changes in tax benefits. Ultimately, though, you'll want to select the IRA that best matches your financial and personal goals. That makes it pretty much your decision. Perhaps the best feature of IRAs is that it's nearly impossible to make a bad choice.

80.

Taxes and Your Stock Portfolio

Let's face it: To become as rich as most of us would like to be, we can't rely on income alone. Our talent and productivity usually won't be rewarded well enough to put us on Easy Street, so we must look to supplement our salary in some way. Ownership of a business—either in whole or through the small pieces of a company that stock brings—makes some sense as a means to this end. Our society tends to reward risk more than it does productivity, and the stock market certainly brings both risks and rewards.

One of the risks of the market is the taxes assessed on your profits. The Tax Code considers these capital gains and taxes them at rates that depend on how long you've held the assets. The actual rates of capital gains taxes are one of the more fluid features of our tax laws, but whether they're up or down in a given year, they're usually lower than the tax rate on ordinary income. That enhances the attractiveness of stocks as investments; you have profit potential, and your profits are taxed more mildly than ordinary income. (You may have state and local taxes on your capital gains, as well; don't overlook these.)

Not all stock investments are successful, of course, but losses come with a silver lining. You can use anything that you lose in the market to offset any passive gains—including profits on stock sales—and lower your tax bill that way.

If you do profit, the capital gains tax applies in the calendar year in which you sell the stocks. This leads many stockholders to key end-of-year decisions. Should you sell the assets and take your profits now, or defer the sale to next year or later? If you sell now and show a profit, do you have passive losses this year to offset the gains? Is the capital gains tax rising, falling, or constant next year, and how will that affect your decisions?

All are legitimate questions; all are a vital part of tax planning that should involve your tax team. But don't let your concerns about capital gains taxes unduly affect your investments. The timing of sales is not unimportant, but the underlying value of your investments is more vital. Focus on the big picture, and let that be your guide to stock acquisition and disposition.

81.

It's the After-Tax Return That Counts

The technology boom of the late twentieth century created a lot of suddenly wealthy people with a new need—profitable vehicles for investment. Even when the Internet bubble burst, it still left many taxpayers with huge reserves of discretionary cash. The investment community had much to say about what to do with this surplus, creating new vehicles, and twists on traditional vehicles, to attract this new wealth.

It was during this period that we saw a great many claims—substantiated or otherwise—promulgated by the operators of mutual funds and other investment vehicles. All the hoopla made for a noisy, confusing investment marketplace.

Many people, intimidated by complex financial matters they don't fully understand, accept claims of investment know-how, expertise, and success at face value. With your growing knowledge and confidence, there's no longer any reason why you should be in that group. Research such claims—and get help from your tax team.

Most funds are required to publish reports about their performance. If you review this publicly available material, it will help you sort the hip from the hype.

As you conduct your research, pay special attention to the after-tax performance of the funds that you're considering. Many times, sales talk will trumpet the gain-before-taxes success of a fund without mentioning the capital gains levy. It's the after-tax performance that counts—that's the true measure of money in your pocket.

With some mutual funds, you may be responsible for taxes on asset sales within the funds, even though the sales took place before you invested in these funds. This distribution of taxes to you, of course, could substantially reduce your after-tax profit for your holdings in such funds.

The keys to evaluating investment opportunities are research and emphasis on after-tax performance. If you reduce all investment possibilities to the common denominator of after-tax returns, you'll have a solid basis for comparison and action.

82.

401(k) Plans—They're Still Okay

In the wake of the corporate failures of the technology era, it was revealed that the 401(k) plans of many employees contained a less-than-diverse portfolio. Many taxpayers saw their retirement savings all but wiped out as the bubble burst and the economy realigned itself. This was devastating for them, and the image of 401(k) plans didn't fare too well, either. Many 401(k) participants began to question the wisdom of their investments.

While personal losses were tragic as many industries regrouped, you shouldn't be dissuaded from investing in a 401(k) plan if your employer offers one. But, the lesson learned is that you do need to actively manage your 401(k) account.

The principal advantage of these plans is their tax-deferral feature. You contribute a portion of your earnings on which you would otherwise pay income taxes. You pay no immediate taxes on your contribution—or on any profits that you realize in your account. All taxes are deferred until much later in your life, when you begin taking distributions from your account. At that point in your life, your income presumably will be less than it is now, so the bite will be smaller than if you were taxed today.

Many employers also have a matching feature; they'll match your contributions, perhaps at a one-to-one rate, perhaps at a rate that's somewhat higher or lower. Again, your taxes on this benefit are deferred.

There are rules for distributions and early withdrawals from your account, and you'll need to consider what to do with your account if you change jobs. You'll want to familiarize yourself with all of the appropriate procedures. The most important thing that you can do to assure the full benefits of your 401(k) plan is to be an active manager.

With most funds, you have many options for moving money within your account. If some of your 401(k) funds are in securities, you have the authority to sell those securities and purchase others. If some of your 401(k) money is in mutual funds, you can leave those funds and invest in others.

You have a great deal of flexibility in managing your 401(k). If you research all of the options and take advantage of that flexibility, you can create a powerful tool for wealth accumulation and tax savings. With 401(k) plans, act as the same proactive team coach that you are on all other tax matters.

83.

The Joker in the Mutual Funds Deck

Few investment categories have grown in popularity so much as mutual funds—and with good reason. Most financial advisors tell us that a diversified portfolio is the key to successful investing. Your risk is spread over many stocks and bonds. If one sector of the economy fizzles, you have limited representation in that sector. The balance of your fund can continue perking along.

There's no disputing this wisdom. Time and again, diversified portfolios have withstood all manner of economic downturns. For that reason, most investors participate in some sort of mutual funds. According to the Investment Company Institute, the combined assets of America's mutual funds in January 2002 totaled nearly seven trillion dollars! But there can be a catch—the way that these funds assign capital gains and losses. If you own an individual security, you control the timing of capital gains and losses by determining when to sell the assets. If you want to realize your gains or losses this calendar year, you sell now. If you want to defer your gains or losses to a future year, you hang onto the assets.

Mutual funds work differently. They regularly buy and sell the securities and bonds within the fund—with no input from you, and no regard for your tax needs. If a mutual fund realizes capital gains on asset sales, you will be assigned a percentage of those gains—even if you weren't a fund participant when the assets were sold. You invest in a mutual fund in November, and you're responsible for the January through October capital gains on asset sales. You say that you weren't around to enjoy the benefits of the asset appreciation? No matter. You're assigned a portion of the capital gains. These unforeseen taxes can wreak havoc with your tax planning and your savings scheme. You won't know how much to save if you can't project what your mutual funds taxes will be.

The solution to this mystery is research. Before investing in mutual funds, you and your tax team should inquire about the potential tax obligation that you might be facing. Touch base with the managers of the funds, and don't be shy about asking specific, pointed questions. If they want your hard-earned money, they should be prepared to level with you about the capital gains taxes that you may be facing.

84.

The Dreaded Alternative
Minimum Tax

For years, the IRS has been concerned about the impact of abusive tax shelters on its ability to collect its fair share of income taxes from each of us. The IRS has attacked the problem in a number of ways—through promotional efforts, through high-profile prosecutions of tax abusers, and through a levy known as the Alternative Minimum Tax (AMT).

Here's the way that the AMT works. When you compute your federal income taxes, you of course factor in all of your credits and deductions, including those designed to help families and the offsets for state and local taxes that you pay. Next, you compute your AMT, this time omitting many of those otherwise allowable deductions and credits. (Use a flat twenty-six percent rate on income up to $175,000, twenty-eight percent on income beyond that.) If your AMT tax obligation is higher than the total that you got through your standard calculations, you're responsible for paying the difference.

This is no small matter. As reported by the Associated Press, Congress' Joint Committee on Taxation estimates that by the year 2010, 35 million taxpayers will be responsible for at least some AMT payments.

The IRS does allow for some exemptions in determining the income that is subject to the AMT. Yet it poses one of the cruelest ironies of the whole tax landscape: The greater your deductions and credits, the more likely it is that you'll be paying the AMT. From time to time, Congress reviews the AMT and tinkers with the exemptions and other aspects of the levy, but it has been loath to eliminate the tax because of the corresponding heavy loss of revenue.

The AMT is one the few tax obligations that doesn't seem amenable to sharp and careful planning. If that's the case, why worry about it? Get over your dread of the AMT. Continue your diligent tax planning, and you'll realize plenty of benefits in other areas.

85.

The Lowdown on Inheritance Taxes

As a nation, our attitude about bequeathing our money to loved ones has been peripatetic. On the one hand, our free enterprise system encourages all workers to make as much money as they can and generate healthy tax payments in the process. Then, if you do just what the system encourages you to do and become wealthy, your income gets whacked by taxes again when you leave it to your heirs.

That's been the paradox of inheritance taxes in America. It may be appropriate for the beneficiary of an estate to pay taxes on inherited income; that dovetails with our notion that income taxes should be based, at least in part, on our ability to pay. Yet this inconsistent attitude about wealth has created some undesirable consequences.

Many heirs have found estate taxes so burdensome—prior to 2001, the hit could be as high as fifty-five percent—that they've had to sell off some of their assets to meet their tax obligations. Sometimes, this means liquidating businesses and eliminating jobs for all employed there.

Congress tried to get its hands around this situation with the passage of the Tax Relief & Reconciliation Act of 2001. The law phases out inheritance taxes by the year 2010. (It does not address the separate inheritance taxes that are levied by many states. For this levy, there may be little relief.)

But the new law doesn't end our inheritance tax concerns. It's scheduled to "sunset" in 2010; if Congress takes no additional action by then, the inheritance tax schedule reverts to its pre-2001 status, bringing back all of the headaches. Many of us hope to be alive and still accumulating wealth by 2010, so the new, relaxed law may not even be in effect by the time that our estates are finally settled.

What this means is that federal inheritance taxes still may be with us when it's time for us to pass the baton, and that comprehensive estate planning still makes sense. It will ease the tax burden on our heirs, and ease the emotional burden on us.

86.

Factoring Taxes
into Estate Planning

As the federal government phases out the inheritance tax, you should experience some relief in efforts at estate planning. Federal taxes have long been the greatest concern in estate planning, particularly for those with significant assets facing a hit up to fifty-five percent. Even with this relief, you'll face other tax implications as you determine how to pass on your wealth and provide for your heirs.

Unfortunately, the federal phase-out will have no impact on state inheritance taxes. These will continue at varying rates. The good news is that the states' demands don't even begin to approximate what the federal tax share has been, so your heirs will emerge with a bigger share of your estate.

A more insidious problem may be unpaid taxes at the time of your death. This doesn't include taxes that you failed to pay through neglect or malice. Rather, it's the bill due on all of those wonderful tax-deferred investments you so sagely purchased along the way.

Remember that 401(k) plan and that IRA that you started years ago? If you haven't taken distributions by the time of your passing, chances are that you haven't paid any of the deferred taxes. You still owe them, and if you die before paying them, the obligation falls to your heirs. You may have been funding these plans for years; if so, the growth in your assets could be spectacular. That could provide a spectacular tax bill for your heirs.

A piece of good news here is that if your spouse is the beneficiary of these investment plans, they may be rolled over into the spouse's name and maintain their tax-deferred status. This is true of most assets—they can be transferred between spouses without triggering any tax obligations. Of course, when the second spouse dies, all of the tax obligations—they could be mountainous by this time—fall upon that spouse's heirs.

These consequences should reinforce the notion that—even with the demise of federal inheritance taxes—estate planning still makes a lot of sense. It's definitely a matter for you and your tax team to consider. It is odd that the savvy investments you make today could be both beneficial and burdensome for your heirs—they will inherit both your wealth and your tax obligations. Planning will help, but the fundamental obligation will remain.

87.

The Joy of Giving

Tis better to give than to receive, the conventional wisdom has it. But in the area of estate planning for tax purposes, you can do both and double your pleasure.

It is true that as a country, our attitude to inherited wealth has been all over the board. First, we heavily tax. Then we declare that all inheritance taxes are to be phased out, except that they can be phased back in unless we say otherwise. To be perfectly frank, ours has not been a model of public policy in the area of inherited wealth.

Throughout the debate and policy evolution, the federal government has recognized that we ought to be able to give at least small portions of our estates to our heirs—while we're alive—without triggering hefty tax bills. This is embodied in the Tax Code, in the provisions known informally as "gifting," an effective way of passing on a portion of your assets while you're alive.

The Tax Code permits you to give gifts of up to $11,000 per year to any beneficiary—family member or not. If the gift is under the $11,000 ceiling, you as the donor pay no gift taxes. And you're not limited to one recipient. Each beneficiary can receive up to $11,000 per year without generating gift taxes for you.

Think of what you can accomplish with an ongoing gifting program over, say, the next twenty years. You can give up to $220,000 to each beneficiary over that entire period without worrying about gift taxes.

Gifting not only works well for you, but it also can work equally as well for your parents. That's where the receiving comes in. Even as you're providing gifts for your kids, your parents can pass on a part of their assets to you while they're alive. They'll be able to see you enjoy the proceeds of their hard work and savvy planning at the same time that you're enjoying your kids getting a kick from your gifts. Gifting programs bring smiles—not taxes—all around.

88.

Click Your Way to the IRS

Taxes have entered the Information Age. A vast treasury of information is available at the IRS web site (www.irs.gov), meaning that instead of waiting for long minutes on the phone to get answers to your questions, you can visit the site and research as many items as you want at your own convenience.

The site offers a news page to keep you posted on current developments. You'll also find specific pages geared to individual filers, retirees and senior citizens, students, the self-employed, and overseas taxpayers; this segmentation helps you get to the sites that are most useful to you without wasting a lot of time. Businesses, charities, government entities, and tax professionals will also find pages targeted to their particular needs.

You'll discover how to contact local IRS facilities, as well as the Taxpayer Advocate Service, and you can click on links to a number of state taxing authorities and certified IRS corporate partners—those helping with such tasks as electronic filing. Also part of the site is a feature that functions very much like a search engine—type in a keyword and you'll get a directory of all pages that match the topic.

Most of the information on the IRS site is available for downloading and printing, although you will need the appropriate software to download pdf files. The site walks you through that free download.

One of the most useful areas of the site is the FAQs—frequently asked questions. Not only is there a general FAQs button, but most of the categories you click on also offer FAQ features focusing on those specific areas of interest. So you have the opportunity to review generally asked questions, as well as those that are more detailed.

There's even an online game, in the form of a quiz show, which helps lead you to an understanding of the free information and services offered by the IRS. Even as you're developing a great new attitude about your taxes, the IRS is doing the same about its approach to taxpayers.

89.

Getting Help from the Government

Our government has a powerful interest in ensuring that we pay our taxes on time and in full. Each time that a taxpayer errs in the computation process or misses a deadline, it can trigger a costly and time-consuming enforcement procedure. Moreover, tax revenue lost to faulty or late returns is that much less money that the government has to spend.

So we and our government have a mutual interest in making sure we get this tax thing right. Many state and local revenue departments staff tax hotlines to take your questions and review concerns about your returns. Even more comprehensive is the information base of the IRS. It's a veritable library of tax information, ranging from the broadest possible topics to those that would affect only a handful of taxpayers.

If you visit www.irs.gov, you'll find more than 300 forms, documents, and pamphlets in downloadable format—all free of charge. If you work for yourself, you may want to review "Self-

Employment Tax" to make sure that you're styling your taxes correctly. If you have a child or parent in day care, "Child and Dependent Care Expenses" is for you.

Facing some long-term healthcare costs? Check out "Medical and Dental Expenses." Wonder what the consequences will be if you miss this year's filing deadline? "Interest and Penalty Information" should be mandatory, if painful, reading. The IRS also offers some of its documents in a Spanish version.

To be sure, a number of the documents are targeted at niche payers. Chances are that you'll never have the need for the "Dyed Diesel Fuel Inspection Notice," and you may find "Deposit Requirements for Railroad Employees" less than compelling reading. But much of this material will be helpful to you now. If your circumstances change next year, it's nice to know that you have easy access to material that will apply to your new situation.

90.

What Happens if You Can't Pay?

Even the most meticulous planners can be caught up in circumstances beyond their control. You encounter a personal or family medical emergency or a dangerous household condition that must be addressed at once, and you find that the only way to finance these unforeseen expenses is to tap the funds that you've been saving for your tax payments. It happens. Life won't necessarily respect the neat borders that we draw around our financial categories. When you find yourself in this situation, it's important to handle the immediate crisis and the ensuing impact on your tax payments—and to keep your planning process in place.

Once you've taken care of the emergency, it's time to turn your attention to your taxes. If you can't pay your federal taxes in full by April 15, the IRS will offer you an installment payment plan, provided you request one by filling out the appropriate form. (You can download it from the IRS web site, www.irs.gov.) The IRS will ask you what date each month you would like to designate as your regular payment date, and they'll advise you to research other alternatives, such as a bank loan.

You'll need to consider several key points about installment plans. First, even if you know that you'll need help paying the bill, it's important to file your return on time. You may be able to reduce your interest and penalty load—you'll still be responsible for those even if your installment plan is approved—with timely filing and application. Remember also that if you're under an installment plan but find that you're entitled to a refund in a subsequent year, the IRS reserves the right to apply that refund to your outstanding balance—and to delinquencies for student loans, child support, and state taxes. You also will be assessed a one-time charge for the processing of your installment plan application.

Those are the technical aspects of installment paying, but the more important element here is the potential damage to your tax attitude. If you can't pay in full this year, don't let that upset your confident, competent approach to tax planning and preparation. Most of us are comfortable with installment payments in other aspects of our lives. Partial credit card payments and monthly insurance premiums are common.

It's preferable to pay in full, if only to avoid the interest and penalty charges that increase the overall bill. But installment paying isn't the end of the world. Think of it as a wakeup call—something that you can avoid in the future with careful planning and better luck.

91.

A Kinder, Gentler IRS

The image of the IRS always has been forbidding. We tend to think of those that work for it as poker-faced bureaucrats, indifferent to our individual circumstances, bound and determined to squeeze every last penny from us.

This intimidating perception is at odds with the way that we view our government. We don't like to think of our elected officials and their appointees running roughshod over us, and the government has demonstrated some sensitivity to this concern.

One result was the 1997 creation of Citizen Advocacy Panels to solicit input on tax policy from the people most affected by that policy, and to convey that information to legislators. Another step forward was creation of the Taxpayer Advocate Service to act as a sort of ombudsman between taxpayers and the IRS.

The Taxpayer Advocate Service is available to help you if an IRS action or proposed action would cause "significant hardship," which is defined as "the immediate threat of adverse action; a delay of more than 30 days in resolving your IRS problems; major costs to you, including fees for professional services, if relief is not granted; irreparable injury or prolonged adverse impact if relief is not granted."

Once the Taxpayer Advocate Service takes on your case, it promises a "fresh look" at your problem, the name and phone number of the person assisting you, updates on progress, time frames for action, and speedy resolution. That's a nice complement of services, indicative of a kinder, gentler IRS, one more interested in collaborating with us than browbeating us.

However, you should be aware that the Taxpayer Advocate Service won't automatically accept your case, and that you must submit an application to be heard. You can download the form from the IRS web site, www.irs.gov; call the IRS forms-only phone number, (800) 829-3676, for an application; or call the Taxpayer Advocate Service's office at (877) 777-4778. You can submit your form online or by fax.

You can see for yourself how the Taxpayer Advocate Service is performing in its ombudsman role. The service's annual reports are available at the IRS web site.

92.

If You Get a Notice, Take Note

In the days before the kinder, gentler IRS, many taxpayers harbored the fear that the "T-Men" would show up at their doors, ready to haul them off for "interviews" that would be conducted in hard-backed chairs with bright lights. This always was a distortion of the power and methods of the IRS, and it's an even more obsolete nightmare now.

If you do hear from the IRS, your initial contact will probably be a written notice, a letter that you receive in the mail. Much of the time, the letter will be to inform you of a simple adjustment to your return. The IRS may have discovered an error in your calculations, a deduction you took that shouldn't have been allowed, or even an error in their own calculations.

The letter will notify you of the recalculation and any adjustment to your tax bill. Sometimes, this will result in additional money due, but it could just as easily bring a credit for you.

In other cases, your notice will cite different errors that are easily corrected. Your Social Security number may be listed incorrectly. You or your tax preparer may have neglected to sign all checks and returns. You may have failed to attach a required supplemental schedule.

If you receive such a notice, take note of it, of course, but don't panic. First, review the contention and any revised calculations by the IRS. If it's helpful, bring members of your tax team into the loop. Should you and your team agree with the IRS, take the necessary corrective action, and you'll be done with this matter.

You also have options if you disagree with the new IRS findings. You can call the Taxpayer Advocate Service—the hotline number is (877) 777-4778—or you can contact the IRS at its general numbers, (800) 829-8815 and (800) 829-1040. Either way, you will be referred to someone who will hear you out.

With notices, proceed as you do on all other tax matters. Be confident, be assertive, and keep records of all communications with the IRS (and any other government entity that you may contact). Resolution of disputes may take time and conversations with a number of officials. If you have complete documentation, the process will be easier for you and the government.

93.

Understanding Types of Audits

Ask people what they fear most about the entire tax process, and they're likely to tell you that it's an audit by the IRS. Most people never have been audited and never will be audited, but the fear is nonetheless real. The fact of the matter is that when the IRS turned kinder and gentler, it modified its auditing procedures, as well.

There was a period when IRS auditing practices could nab taxpayers through no fault of those taxpayers. This occurred through the service's Taxpayer Compliance Measurement Program, which audited thousands of taxpayers on a randomly selected basis to help establish norms for deductions and expenses. The program raised such protests that it was abandoned in 1995. Periodically, the IRS undertakes random audit projects, as it did in 2002, but as a rule, your federal tax return won't be randomly audited.

The IRS does maintain three types of regular audits. Correspondence audits usually cover routine matters and generally are handled by mail. Office audits may involve more complex matters; you and your representative will be invited to the local IRS office to discuss them. The field audit is a more thorough review involving larger amounts of money—unreported income typically is the focus—and is basically reserved for businesses.

All three types of audits are for what the IRS considers cause—something about your return that throws up a red flag. If you fail to respond to IRS correspondence, that could raise their attention level. Casualty losses, foreign bank accounts, a huge prospective refund—all are phenomena that could mark your return for auditing.

Yet another red flag would be a mismatch between the income that you've reported and what your employers and clients say that they've paid you. The IRS matches up both sides of the earnings equation via computer and is likely to be aware of any discrepancies.

If you're the subject of an audit of any kind—states and municipalities conduct tax audits, as well—treat it seriously, but don't fear this specter inordinately. If you and your tax team are following all procedures carefully, an audit isn't likely to reveal anything untoward.

Once the IRS halted random reviews, the chances of any taxpayer being audited became pretty small. Figures compiled by the West Group in their publication, *Representing the Audited Taxpayer Before the IRS*, show that in 1998, the IRS audited 0.99 percent of all individual returns filed and 2.09 percent of corporate returns filed. The percentages—and the efficiency of your tax team—are in your favor.

94.

Thou Shalt Fear No Audit

If you do receive notice of an audit—from the IRS or any taxing body—don't panic. You're well beyond that sort of irrational reaction, because you've been planning your taxes carefully and documenting every action. If the government wants to review your filing, that's okay, because you're prepared.

Knowing the standard procedures in audits and your rights as a taxpayer also will help you approach your audit with confidence. Make sure that your accountant or other tax preparer briefs you on both of these key items.

If you're contacted for a correspondence audit, huddle with your tax team to hammer out a draft response. Review the draft as a team, and finalize it as a team.

If it's an office audit, note on your calendar the date and time for your audit, and then proceed in the same way as you would with a correspondence audit. Develop a plan of action with your tax team, making sure to solicit input from all members. You're the coach, so the final approach is up to you.

You always have the right to appeal any audit findings, and you have some procedural flexibility, as well. To dispute the findings of a correspondence audit, for example, you may request an interview or appeals conference. For office audits, you can propose a date other than the one requested by the IRS, and you're not required to attend the meeting in most cases. If you find that your appeals have stalled out, you always have the option of contacting the Taxpayer Advocate Service, which should get the ball rolling again.

Even though you're the coach of your tax team, many practitioners in this area suggest than if an office audit is involved, you should elect not to attend. Stay home. Let your accountant handle the meeting and update you as soon as it's over.

The thinking here is that many of us, nervous about the proceedings and unaccustomed to being interviewed by a federal official, will respond emotionally rather than rationally and raise the animosity level at the audit. Does that sound like you? If it does, this may be one game that the coach can win by staying on the bench.

95.

Pitching Your Files? Not So Fast

If you're like most of us, you probably have limited space for files in your home. You have one file cabinet that's already overflowing, spilling over into an orange crate that you've saved as a makeshift file repository. The temptation is strong to pitch your tax documents every few years to create space for new files—and to give you a sense that your obligations for those years finally are over.

Work hard to resist this temptation. There are compelling reasons for hanging onto your tax files. The most obvious of these is the possibility of an audit by a taxing body. The IRS can audit your returns for up to three years, and they don't have to cite a reason for doing so. If they believe that you have an outstanding tax obligation, the time limit for audits is six years. If they suspect something more devious than a simple underpayment, like fraud, there is no time limit or statute of limitations.

So if your tax returns have ever been subject to auditing by the IRS, it stands to reason that you should preserve your records for as long as is feasible. Without supporting documents, you will be left to reconstruct decades-old earnings and payments histories from memory, which is a faulty vessel at best.

Another good reason for hanging onto your tax records is that they can be a valuable tool in helping you track the performance of your investments. Let's say that you've invested in a mutual fund. At the end of each year, the fund will send you a report of gains, losses, and taxes paid during the year. The primary purpose, of course, is to give you a record of your taxes. But they're also providing you with a year-to-year performance record for the fund. If you preserve and review these records, you'll have a clear picture of how your fund is performing over time—and whether you should be thinking about reallocating your money. For this reason, it's best to retain your tax records for as long as you're involved with the investments reported on those records.

The bottom line is this: You can pitch relatively recent files and their potentially valuable information, or you can buy another small filing cabinet. Go with the cabinet. Your twenty-dollar investment could save you tons in the long run.

96.

Enjoy That Refund

Successfully completing and submitting your tax returns is a cause for celebration; receiving a refund due to overpayment is another reason to cut loose. You've been diligent all year, controlling your spending so that you could stay on budget, meticulously preserving and filing records of earnings and expenses, and communicating regularly with your tax preparer and other members of your tax team.

How should you celebrate your refund? Do whatever it is that would give you the most pleasure. Here are some ideas.

- Take a loved one to dinner and a movie.
- Take your team to lunch.
- Enjoy a romantic vacation weekend with your significant other.
- Give the kids a one-time premium in their allowance.
- Get your dog a bag of ridiculously overpriced treats.

- License that pricey software package that you've been fantasizing about.

- Donate a little something extra to your favorite charity.

Some people will be most satisfied indulging some long-repressed desire. Others will take more pleasure in financing a noble civic effort. It's your refund, you decide. It's feel-good time.

97.

Take the Long View on Tax Cuts

During the political season, it's common to hear elected officials and their challengers try to outdo each other in their pledges for tax relief. There's a tendency to respond to these initiatives with your own pocketbook—that is, to support the tax measures that appear to bring the greatest benefits for you. As appealing as this may sound, it may be a shortsighted approach that can hurt you—and all of us—in the long run.

Think about your best financial years. If you're like most of us, those cushy periods occurred when the American economy was percolating and good times were widespread, not restricted to a privileged group or two. It's axiomatic but still often overlooked—when America is prospering generally, Americans generally are prospering.

Think about that as you mull over your support for the inevitable tax proposals. If you take the global perspective on tax policy, you'll probably back the proposals that make the most sense for the larger community. The pennies will inevitably trickle down to you.

98.

Plan for the Long Term

One of the great benefits of becoming competent and confident in the tax arena is that you're now able to consider taxes in your long-term planning. Certainly, you can take this year's refund and spend it on something that provides immediate gratification. There's no harm in that. You worked hard for it, so go ahead, spend it as you see fit— even frivolously if you choose—and don't feel guilty about it.

Even as you do, however, remember that it's important to take a longer view of tax planning. Don't look at it as a battle that begins and ends each April 15. The stakes are higher than that. Think of tax planning and preparation as a vehicle for continuing benefits—one that can help you in all your financial decisions.

You can, for example, utilize your knowledge of taxes in development of your investment portfolio, factoring the tax implications of each potential investment into your buy/sell decisions. You now know how to manage the funds in your 401(k) account and which IRA is best for your circumstances—and which will be best if your situation changes. This knowledge can be an important contributor to the growth of your savings and the achievement of your personal and professional goals.

You understand the tax implications of homeownership and home improvements, and you're conversant with the tax issues associated with kids—the expenses that you can deduct, the taxes on their income. Wherever taxes come into play on the family front, you're on top of them.

Your familiarity with taxes also will help you plan your estate, preserving as much of it as possible for your heirs and even allowing you to see your beneficiaries enjoy your gifts while you're alive. That's a major benefit.

Remember when you dreaded the mere mention of taxes, wanting to farm out all of your preparation so that you wouldn't have to think of the "T- word"? You've come a long way since then. You know taxes now, and you're ready to put that competence to work over the balance of your life. Tax planning will become an effective force in your future.

99.

Taxation with Representation

When our forefathers went to war against the British, one of the most popular battle cries was, "No taxation without representation." The courage and success of those freedom fighters helped pave the way for our representative democracy. We've enjoyed that type of government for more than 300 years, and if the truth be known, we probably take it for granted more than we should.

What we have now is taxation *with* representation—that is, we elect officials at various levels of government to reflect our wishes in all areas of policy, including taxes. We've grown as a nation since those formative years, so much that we sometimes lose sight of the representative role of our government. The principal job of the members of our government remains to represent us; to do that job properly, our legislators need to know how we think about the issues before them.

Do you believe that your school taxes are too low to support the kind of quality education that your community needs? Pick up the phone, and call your school board member. A direct phone call is an appropriate way to communicate at the local level. You can also call your local council. Almost invariably, your council representative will have a staff person to take your call—and pass along your thoughts to the elected official.

At the state and federal levels, where districts tend to be larger, it would be unreasonable to expect your legislator to take your call personally. There wouldn't be enough hours in the day for these legislators to handle all constituent calls directly. But you can send a letter or fire off an e-mail expressing your views. If you do send a letter, don't worry about having it professionally produced on letterhead stationery. That's not necessary. A handwritten note that's long on genuine feeling can be even more persuasive than a professionally styled missive.

Think about forming or adding your name to petitions for tax-related matters. There's no danger in signing a petition that accurately reflects your views. It's one more way of assuring that your legislators get your message—and that we have responsive representation on taxation.

100.

Look Forward to Next Year

One of the great benefits of successfully completing your tax returns—on time and accurately—is that you now have a process that you can repeat year after year. The numbers will change, and the documents will vary, but you have institutionalized your tax process and can complete it without undue stress. Where taxes are concerned, you're habitual rather than hyper, predictable rather than panic-stricken.

Think of your accomplishments in the tax area. You've created a team of dedicated, experienced professionals to lead your tax charge. You've implemented a budgeting and accrual program to ensure that you have enough funds to pay any tax bills. You've devised a communications network so that all parties involved in your taxes are in the loop. You understand the tax implications of all of your major financial choices, including your home and investment portfolio. You've developed an annual plan for aiding your favorite civic and charitable groups.

In short, you no longer stress about taxes because you realize that when looked at from the proper perspective, it's all stuff that you can handle. Remember when just the mention of taxes activated your anxiety meter? When you couldn't think rationally about taxes because it was an uncomfortable and emotional subject for you? That's not you anymore.

In fact, it wouldn't be a surprise if you were actually looking forward to calculating your taxes for next year. Your competence and attitude have empowered you. When you find that contemplating next year's tax drill gives you just that hint of satisfaction, you know that your journey is complete.